THE GROWN-UP'S GUIDE TO TEENAGE HUMANS

Praise for
THE GROWN-UP'S GUIDE TO TEENAGE HUMANS

"This is an invaluable guide to understanding, influencing, and genuinely helping the teenager in your life. Josh offers uncompromisingly practical tips to restore trust, build mutual respect, and expertly help them navigate adolescence successfully."
—Rosalind Wiseman, *New York Times* bestselling author of *Queen Bees and Wannabes* and founder of Cultures of Dignity

"An essential guide to understanding and positively influencing adolescents. This book is equal parts inspiring and genuinely helpful for every parent, youth worker, educator, or anyone involved with teens in any capacity."
—Salome Thomas-EL, award-winning principal and author of *The Immortality of Influence*

"As both a mom and a professor, I found this parenting book to be a breath of fresh air. Josh skillfully combines heart, humor, and research-backed strategies to reclaim harmony with the teenage human in your life."
—Kimberly Allen, PhD, Department of Youth, Family, and Community Sciences at North Carolina State University

"I've devoted my career to helping business leaders skillfully navigate situations where the stakes are high, opinions vary, and emotions run strong. Never is that more true than when you're a parent. Josh's data-backed insights give parents the words to say and the mindset to embody for this crucial window of influence with our own kids."
—Joseph Grenny, coauthor of *New York Times* bestseller *Crucial Conversations*

"Raising an accountable adult is challenging but possible. Josh Shipp presents practical solutions to help parents and other caring adults be as effective as possible, even in the most difficult situations. You will acquire new strategies to provide teens with the skills and confidence they need to be successful!"

—John G. Miller, author of QBQ! The Question Behind the Question
and Raising Accountable Kids

"As a dad I appreciate how practical Josh's insights are. This book provides effective and practical ways to handle even the most squirmworthy moments of the teenage years."

—Doyin Richards, fatherhood advocate and contributor
to Upworthy and Parents magazine

"Teenagers pose unique challenges for parents, teachers, and caregivers. This book is an essential read, providing a unique pathway to best understand, connect with, and guide us in nurturing healthy, resilient teens."

—Gene Beresin MD, MA, executive director of The Clay
Center for Young Healthy Minds and professor of
psychiatry at Harvard Medical School

"Research keeps telling us that committed adults make a difference in the lives of teenagers. Now, Josh Shipp tells you how to be that adult. The Grown-Up's Guide to Teenage Humans is a must-have resource for anyone who has a heart for the next generation."

—Dave Ramsey, bestselling author and nationally
syndicated radio show host

"The world needs this book. Few have the insight or ability to share life-changing words like Josh does. Here he provides a look at how we can all help shape the lives of the people most important to us. He does so in typical Josh Shipp fashion: with equal parts humor and heart."   —Brad Montague, creator of Kid President

"This book is the training manual you never got. A must-have resource for parents, teachers, or anyone else who has to deal with teens." —Ellen Rakieten, executive producer of *Oprah*

"The success and impact of my work originates with teachers and other caring adults who invested in me during my formative teen-age years. Josh Shipp's book arms caring adults with the principles, insights, and inspiration they need to help teens they care about succeed."

—Jack Canfield, cocreator of the Chicken Soup for the Soul® series and author of *The Success Principles*™

"This book provides a deep understanding of a teenager's needs and a practical guide for nurturing optimal development. The advice Josh shares is evidence-based, no-nonsense, and uncompromising in its practicality. These insights will teach us how we can be that one caring adult every teen needs."

—Julie Lythcott-Haims, author of *New York Times* bestseller *How to Raise an Adult*

"An accessible primer for helping parents understand and guide their kids through the often-confounding adolescent years. Shipp addresses an array of typical problems faced by adolescents, each one accompanied by simple and logical action steps."

—*Publishers Weekly*

"Shipp commands our attention as he gives us advice about dealing with our teenagers. . . . How to create trust and mutual respect is the meat of this book. . . . *The Grown-Up's Guide to Teenage Humans* resonates deeply and contains some amazing stories. . . . Sometimes it's a simple idea that leaves you with goose bumps: a kid's life can be transformed by a caring adult who's just a little bit more bullheaded than the kid." —*New York Times Book Review*

ALSO BY JOSH SHIPP

The Teen's Guide to World Domination

Jump Ship

THE GROWN-UP'S GUIDE TO TEENAGE HUMANS

How to Decode Their Behavior,
Develop Trust, and Raise a
Respectable Adult

Josh Shipp

HARPER WAVE

An Imprint of HarperCollins*Publishers*

This manuscript was written with my dear and brilliant friend David A. Tieche.

A hardcover edition of this book was published in 2017 by Harper Wave, an imprint of HarperCollins Publishers.

FIRST HARPER WAVE PAPERBACK EDITION PUBLISHED 2018.

Library of Congress Cataloging-in-Publication Data

Names: Shipp, Josh, author.

Title: The grown-up's guide to teenage humans : how to decode their behavior, develop unshakable trust, and raise a respectable adult / Josh Shipp.

Description: First edition. | New York, NY : HarperCollins, 2017.

Identifiers: LCCN 2017018931 (print) | LCCN 2017029731 (ebook) | ISBN 978-0-06-265408-3 (eBook) | ISBN 978-0-06-265406-9 (hardcover) | ISBN 978-0-06-269593-2 (audio)

Subjects: LCSH: Parent and teenager. | Teenagers and adults. | Teenagers. | Adolescence.

Classification: LCC HQ799.15 (ebook) | LCC HQ799.15 .S565 2017 (print) | DDC 306.874—dc23

LC record available at https://lccn.loc.gov/2017018931

ISBN 978-0-06-265407-6 (pbk.)

20 21 22   LSC   10 9 8 7

To Isaiah, my favorite teenage human: I'm proud of you.

CONTENTS

Part 1: THE THREE KEY MINDSETS

Part 2: THE PHASES OF A TEENAGE HUMAN

Part 3: TROUBLESHOOTING COMMON TEENAGE CHALLENGES

Resources from Josh

THE GROWN-UP'S GUIDE TO TEENAGE HUMANS

This book aims to help grown-ups who care for and interact with teens.

You may be their parent,* teacher, coach, or grandmother.

They may be your kid, student, athlete, or grandson.

In an effort to write this book as prescriptively as possible, much of the advice and many of the situations are aimed at parents. However, the ideas can be customized to nearly any caring adult's unique situation and relationship.

So for the rest of the book, let's use this shorthand, shall we?

Parent = any parent, educator, coach, mentor, or caring adult. In essence, *you.*

Your teen(s) = any teen(s) in your classroom, home, or care.

Thanks for doing what you do. It's my deepest hope that this book helps you.

---

* Perhaps you thought a baby would be a nice addition to the family, only you didn't consider that baby would someday turn into a teenager.

EVERY KID NEEDS A "RODNEY"

Statistically, I am supposed to be dead, in jail, or homeless. Because I was a foster kid, my odds were already pretty bleak. About 20 percent of foster kids end up homeless. Less than 3 percent go on to earn a college degree. Only about half will be gainfully employed by the time they turn twenty-four years old.

In addition to that, I was actively working to worsen my already bad situation. I was stubborn. I was making stupid choices. I was marvelously bitter. All at the ripe old age of fourteen.

So what happened?

Rodney happened.

Before I moved in with Rodney, I had mastered the art of getting kicked out of foster homes with dizzying speed. I was like a lone wolf version of the von Trapp kids, driving away foster parents with my antics.

Yes, I just made a *Sound of Music* reference, and the point is this: Getting kicked out was my goal. In fact, I was so callous and removed from my situation that I made it a game. I actually kept a logbook—a Mead journal composition book with a black-and-white mottled cover—in which I would log the stats of how quickly I could get kicked out of each foster home.

Column 1: The date I entered the home.

Column 2: The date I was kicked out.

Column 3: The strategy I employed for getting kicked out.

The goal: Beat my high score, which at the time was less than a week.

The truth is, I was terrified, and my logbook gave me a sense of control. Because what kids don't talk out, they will act out.

I trusted no one. Especially adults. My birth parents had abandoned me when I was born, which is how I ended up as a ward of the state of Oklahoma. And because my first set of adults broke my trust by not sticking around, I unfairly assumed that all subsequent adults would do the same.

One night while I was living in a group foster care home, one of the older boys snuck into our room and raped some of the younger boys. Including me. No one stopped that horror from happening. No one stepped in.

It's tough for kids to live in a world where they believe that no adult is going to look out for them. It creates a terrible anxiety and loneliness, and everything feels uncertain.

It's hard to handle this kind of weight. At one point in my preteen years, I was bullied so much and felt so alone and worthless that I tried to end my life by taking a bottle of pills. I couldn't fathom a world in which I could trust anyone.

Again: What kids don't talk out, they will act out.

That was when Rodney happened.

One of the odd things about being a foster kid is that new "parents" are randomly bestowed upon you. Ten minutes earlier, these people were complete strangers. And then, ten minutes later, some social worker says, "Josh, meet your new mom and dad."

I showed up on Rodney's doorstep the summer before my seventh-grade year. I was fourteen years old, and I had lots of baggage. Not luggage—emotional baggage. Fourteen years of stuff that clearly wasn't Rodney's fault, though now it was his issue.

At first glance, Rodney seemed as though he was going to be an easy victory for me. He had no special psychological training. He had no certification for dealing with highly oppositional teens like me. He had no obvious or overwhelming skill or talent. He was just a portly midwestern man, shaped like a lowercase B, who happened to have narcolepsy. I'm not making that up. Sometimes Rodney would just fall asleep with no warning. Like when your cable goes out inexplicably. He'd be awake, and then, night night.

This was sure to be my easiest opponent to date.

My well-meaning social worker gave me some parting advice—something along the lines of "Give these nice folks a chance, would you? Also, remember arson is illegal." I moved into Rodney's house and immediately began to implement my game plan: get kicked out of here ASAP.

I began with my typical opening overtures. I was obnoxious. I was defiant. I was ungrateful. I was rude. I stole Doritos from the school store. I got suspended from school for public intoxication on school grounds. I got suspended for the second time for hacking into the school's computer files to try to change my grades. I set things on fire. I stole Rodney's Ford Ranger pickup for a joy ride. I was a menace. A whirling dervish of mischief. This was some of my best work to date.

Three. Years. Later.

I couldn't shake this guy. Rodney simply refused to kick me out.

This pissed me off.

But remember that I am a foster kid, which means I'd developed a certain brand of perseverance. After all, perseverance is merely stubbornness with a purpose. And now I had a purpose. Rodney was being stubborn, so I had to step up my game. Tip the scales.

I discovered there was a small town bank in Yukon, Oklahoma, where I could open a checking account. I deposited about $100 into the account. I then proceeded to write $10,000 or so of hot checks. I figured by the time the checks didn't clear, I'd be in the clear. One of those hot checks was a payment for my car insurance. If you don't have car insurance in Oklahoma, the Oklahoma DMV will suspend your driver's license.

I was traveling to Stillwater, Oklahoma, up Interstate 35, where the speed limit was 65 mph. Going at least 85 mph, I raced past a police officer. I had no insurance and no valid driver's license. I was handcuffed and thrown into the back of the cop car and taken to jail.

I was on my way to becoming yet another statistic.

Now, once you are booked, you are allowed that one phone call. I called Rodney.

ME: Rodney.
RODNEY: Yeah.
ME: It's me. Uhhhh, listen. I don't exactly know how to say this, but I did something stupid. I'm in jail in Stillwater. I'll explain everything later. Will you come bail me out?
RODNEY: (*Long pause*)
ME: Rodney? Rodney!? (*I assumed the narcolepsy had kicked in*)
RODNEY: Josh, I will come bail you out. But not until tomorrow. Good-bye. (*Click*)

I was so mad. But Rodney, who was a history teacher and middle school football coach, had a mantra he lived by. "Don't bail a kid out of failure or success, 'cause you learn from both."

The next morning Rodney arrived to bail me out of jail. Just as he said he would. The drive home was incredibly awkward. And keep in mind, I'd just spent the night in jail with strangers. You don't make small talk with the other nice folks in custody when you're seventeen years old.

As we pulled into the driveway, Rodney reached his arm up to pull himself out of the car and said, "We need to sit down and talk."

And that's when I knew. Finally, after three years, I'd succeeded. I'd cracked Rodney. I mentally began to pack my things and make a new entry in my logbook.

Let me be clear: I didn't blame Rodney for wanting to kick me out. He was gracious and really tried. He inconvenienced himself for me.

And I in return was ungrateful, unreasonable, and downright mean. Frankly, I would have wanted to kick me out as well.

Rodney and his wife, Christine, sat me down in the living room to begin the conversation I had heard so many times before.

RODNEY: Josh. You can keep causing trouble, keep pushing us away, keep acting out (*his tone changes*), but you gotta get it through your thick head, son. We don't see you as a problem. We see you as an opportunity.

Then silence.

"Oh, no," I thought, "he's lecturing me. I would rather be kicked out than be subjected to this cheesy motivational speech."

But immediately after that, a different wave of emotions came crashing through my cynicism. I realized that Rodney had proven his resolve. He'd been consistent and committed. He'd been given the case file of my life—with all of its marks and blemishes—and he had seen what no prior adult had been able to detect.

He realized what I could be.

We don't see you as a problem. We see you as an opportunity.

Those words marked my turning point.

*   *   *

You don't have to be a foster kid to face seemingly insurmountable challenges these days:

3.2 million of our teens are being bullied each year.

Fifteen percent of all teens reported having been electronically bullied, and nearly 20 percent said they were bullied at school in the past year.

1.2 million of our teens are dropping out of school each year.

That's seven thousand students dropping out a day. And almost 25 percent of all incoming freshmen will not graduate on time.

Our teens are numbing out with drugs.

Nine out of ten adult addicts began using before they turned eighteen.

Our teens are making dangerous decisions.

Twenty-two percent of students nationwide had been offered, sold, or given an illegal drug by someone on school property during the last twelve months. Just under 17 percent of teens had carried a weapon on at least one day during the last month.

Our teens often feel hopeless.

More than 30 percent of students nationwide reported that they had felt so sad or hopeless almost every day for two or more weeks in a row that they stopped doing some of their usual activities.

And tragically, our teens are killing themselves.

Suicide is the second leading cause of death for fifteen- to twenty-four-year-olds. Each day in our nation there are on average over 5,400 suicide attempts by young people in grades seven through twelve.

These statistics are not taken from communities that lack resources or are poor or otherwise struggling. They represent data from across all communities: Single-parent households. Two-parent households. Wealthy, middle-class, below the poverty line. This is the state of the teenage union. And every teen is one decision away from being a statistic.

Statistically, I should be dead, in jail, or homeless. And yet I'm not. Why?

I am not a statistic because of one caring adult. One imperfect yet deeply committed, caring adult named Rodney.

But please understand. This is not just an anecdotal, inspirational, feel-good story about one kid who got turned around. Let me show you what the folks at Harvard University found.

The Research About Rodneys*

Harvard University developed the Center on the Developing Child with the goal of figuring out how to improve what they call "child outcomes." They set out to study resilience. What enables some kids to make it through tough challenges and causes other kids to fold? What's the common denominator in kids who end up a success story?

Here are their findings:

The single most common factor for children who develop resilience is at least one stable and committed relationship with a supportive parent, caregiver, or other adult. These relationships provide the personalized responsiveness, scaffolding, and protection that buffer children from developmental disruption. They also build key capacities—such as the ability to plan, monitor, and regulate behavior—that enable children to respond adaptively to adversity and thrive.[1]

This social science research from one of the most well-respected universities in the world ratifies what you and I instinctively know from our own lives.

Every kid is one caring adult away from being a success story.

Every kid needs a "Rodney."

Who Was Your Rodney?

You had a Rodney, didn't you? Someone who saw the best in you even when you didn't deserve it. Someone who was *for* you. Someone who

---

* There's a great deal of fascinating research showing the honest-to-goodness impact just one caring adult can make. If you're someone who likes to "nerd out" on this sort of stuff (like me), follow the trail of endnotes to page 297.

called you on the carpet when you needed it. And someone who listened to you when life beat you down. You are the person you are because of that Rodney.

The goal of this book is to help you become the best "Rodney" possible.

Here's what I know when it comes to actually helping your teenager: I'm no match for you. No one is.

I could never even come close to having the impact that you can have in the life of your teen. But I do know something about teens, and I can help. At the risk of sounding like I'm trying to list items from my résumé to gain your trust and confidence, here are some items from my résumé to gain your trust and confidence:

- Over the past decade, I've spoken to more than two million teenagers and caring adults globally. I've made it my life's mission to help adults understand teens and teens understand themselves.

- My work helping troubled teens was made into a documentary TV series called *Teen Trouble* that aired on Lifetime and A&E.

- I've been featured on *Oprah*, *Good Morning America*, and *20/20*, and in the *New York Times* and countless other media outlets to provide insights on teens.

- My organization One Caring Adult provides practical resources to empower parents, teachers, and caring adults around the globe.

- In my entire life, I have never, ever lost a game of Connect Four.

But in addition to all that, I have a personal stake in this. I am a parent of two kids, London and Katie. There are times when, despite my professional knowledge, I feel entirely ill equipped to be the kind of parent I want to be. There are times when I lose my temper, when I act out of my own insecurities, when I'm a complete idiot. There are times when my immaturity has caused me to behave in ways that go against every bit of advice I've put in this book. And yet I desperately want to be a good parent. I want to do whatever I can to help launch my kids into the world so that they're respectable adults.

Now, I don't know you personally, but because you're reading this book, I do know this about you: You want to be a better caring adult. And you're hoping this book will help you toward that end.

The Goal of this Book: Hope and Practical Strategies

In preparing to write this book, my team and I found that the number one critique of books about caring for kids is that they were "too philosophical and not practical enough."

I find this just as frustrating as you do. There's nothing worse than being told that you need to do something but having no idea how to do it. We wanted this book to provide real hope and real strategies that work. To that end, this book is made up of three parts:

Part 1: The Three Key Mindsets
The first three chapters are focused on three major insights that my team and I have found from studying effective parents, educators, coaches, and caring adults. These are three paradigm-shifting Big Ideas you need to adopt if you're going to influence teenagers. This section will provide you with hope and help you stay encouraged as you navigate what it means to be a parent.

Part 2: The Phases of a Teenage Human
Teens are rapidly changing humans. With the help of an incredible team of researchers, psychologists, and scientists, and a massive focus group of caring adults, we've distilled the best information about teenagers down to easy-to-read and easy-to-digest snapshots. These snapshots outline the particular changes that teenagers undergo at every age from eleven through eighteen. We'll also outline exactly what teens need from grown-ups at each stage and the key

actions you can take. This section will help you decode your teen's behavior and needs.

Part 3: Troubleshooting Common Teenage Challenges
A "choose your own adventure" list of issues and situations that you will likely face, along with instructions on how to help your teen successfully navigate those minefields so that they (and you) make it to adulthood more happy, more whole, and more healthy. This section includes step-by-step guidance, scripts to follow, and best practices gleaned from decades of experience from some of the world's top experts to help you have a dramatic impact on your teenagers' lives.

Be a Rodney

Let me be the first to thank you for being the kind of adult who cares about teenagers. Teenagers are amazing almost grown-ups, with swirls of both blazing insecurities and shocking giftedness. They are filled with stunningly beautiful promise, looking forward into impossibly bright futures, and yet they somehow forget to put on shoes before they walk out of the house. And dealing with teens means coping with both sides of the same coin.

In my office, I have a plaque that reads: "I believe the children are our future. Teach them well, and let them lead the way."

I have another plaque that reads: "I believe I can fly."

And another that says, "Don't stop believing."

Truthfully, I don't have any of those signs. But I should. Because they're true. Caring about teens and actively working to make their lives better really matters. And this is not just feel-good Hallmark movie sentimentality. It's hard-as-nails truth. There's a reason I'm so passionate about this. It's because this is my story. I'm living proof of the difference that one caring adult can make in the life of a teenager.

We need to be the kind of adults who help teenagers achieve as much of their potential as they possibly can. We need to protect the fragile nature of their giftedness, and provide environments and spaces where teens can flourish.

Thanks for stepping up to the plate. It takes unbridled optimism to do what you're doing. I hope this book provides you with some encouragement and some practical strategies.

Every kid needs a Rodney. So please: Be a Rodney.

> *Every kid is one caring adult away*
> *from being a success story.*

Part 1

THE THREE KEY MINDSETS

When your kids were little, you were often physically exhausted. Now that they're teens, you're often mentally exhausted. More worry. More arguments. More mental chess.

So how can you stay effective and clinically sane?

Of the thousands of parents and caring adults I've worked with, interviewed, and studied, those who are most effective have a deep understanding of the following three mindsets:

- Teens need you more than it seems.
- The game has changed and so must you.
- You'll want and need help.

Let's learn from them, shall we?

TEENS NEED YOU MORE THAN IT SEEMS

I was ten years old, and nearly all the other boys my age were eagerly waiting for that precise moment when they would be tall enough to ride the Texas Giant, one of the fastest and longest wooden roller coasters in the world.

I sharply deduced—using the power of my advanced ten-year-old mind—that the screaming coming from the cars meant this was no ordinary amusement ride. No! I knew what the adults around me were too enthralled to comprehend: that this roller coaster was actually a wooden death machine, designed to throw me and those around me to our graphic deaths.

I stood in line next to Mrs. Sperry, a family friend who had graciously offered to take me to Six Flags with her kids. I marveled that this woman—who was a teacher and public servant at my local elementary school—could be so cavalier with my young life.

I thought about yelling for help, but clearly I was in a line with other foolish human lemmings, slowly pacing their way toward the wooden death machine. So I got on the Texas Giant next to Mrs. Sperry.

And then I realized something else.

There were no seat belts.

There was simply a lap bar. A single piece of metal that came down and locked across your lap.

I looked around in incredulous wonder.

No seat belts? No five-point harnesses? Did everyone around me have a death wish?

I tugged at the bar. I yanked at it. I tried to stand up to force it to open. I pushed it and tested it, pulled at it with both hands.

Now, did I push and prod and test that lap bar because I was hoping that it would fail? That the springs would release and I would be launched off the Texas Giant to my untimely and graphic death?

Of course not.

I did all that because I needed to confirm that it would hold.

Your teen is doing the exact same thing.

Teenagers will test you to see if you, like the lap bar on a roller coaster, will hold.

They are testing you and prodding you and pushing you because they need to know, at a time when so many other things are uncertain, that YOU are certain.

That you are steady.

That you are safe.

That you will hold.

What Teenagers Want and Need Most

A YMCA Teen and Parent Survey conducted by the Global Strategy Group[2] found that the top concern of teenagers (outpacing all other fears and concerns) was . . .

. . . wait for it . . .

"not having enough time together with their parents."

What?!

You're probably thinking, "This simply cannot be true. I thought that their number one concern was avoiding me at all costs."

Surprisingly, having quality family time concerned teens more than anything else.[3] More than grades. More than friends. More than whether Rebecca will forgive Sean for kissing Desirée. And the survey showed that teens of all ages are concerned by the lack of quality time with their parents.

Conversely, parents are more concerned by outside threats (such as drugs or alcohol) than they are about time spent together. For parents, lack of quality time comes in as the fourth most concerning priority.

But what if the thing your teen needs most is the preventive measure you've been looking for?

Starting in 1990,* an organization called the Search Institute began doing research into children and teens. Specifically, they were interested in attempting to answer the question "Why do some young people develop into successful, contributing adults—and some don't?"

Why do some youth beat the odds in difficult situations and environments, and others get trapped? What's going on?

Data collected from more than five million children and teens from all backgrounds and situations consistently revealed something surprising. What mattered was what the Search Institute calls assets. Half of these assets were internal, meaning positive character traits and values. And the other half were external, meaning positive environments and experiences. The research clearly shows that the more assets a kid has, the more likely he or she will succeed. Some of the assets include** the following:

EXTERNAL ASSETS:
Positive Environments and Experiences

- Family support: Family displays high levels of support and love.
- Service to others: Young person does community service one hour or more per week.

---

* Before cell phones, Google, and even *NSync. I know. Ancient.

** This research is fascinating. I don't want to bog you down in the weeds of it, but if you want, you can find the list of all forty developmental assets by checking out "40 Developmental Assets for Adolescents" at the Search Institute website: search-institute.org.

- Boundaries: Family and school both have clear rules and consequences.
- Constructive use of time: Young person spends time each week in creative arts, sports, youth activities, religious communities, or at home.

INTERNAL ASSETS:
Positive Character Traits and Values

- Commitment to learning: Young person is motivated to do well in school and is actively engaged in his/her education.
- Integrity: Young person has convictions and stands up for them.
- Planning and decision-making: Young person knows how to plan ahead and make choices.
- Positive view of personal future: Young person is optimistic about his or her personal future.

Here are the findings of the Search Institute put simply: The more internal and external assets teens acquire, the better their chances of succeeding.

> *Positive Environments + Positive Character Traits = Success**

---

* In fact, in a Search Institute longitudinal study, researchers found that kids who were of an ethnic minority, lived with a single parent, qualified for free and reduced lunch, and had thirty-one to forty assets were more likely to do better than a white teenager who had two middle-or-upper-income parents but had only ten assets or fewer.

Where You Come In

Think about your own teenage years. Think about the grown-ups in your life who mattered most to you and who most impacted you. That coach. That teacher. That family member.

What do all those people have in common? I would argue they intentionally sacrificed for your benefit.

They went out of their way to encourage you. They consistently showed up. They were grown-ups you respected. They made it clear that they were there for you. They pushed you to do more than you thought you could. And this is the underlying message behind the data collected from the Search Institute's five million surveys.

Positive character traits exist because caring adults have cultivated them.

Positive environments exist because caring adults have cultivated them.

These things don't fall from space. They don't magically appear like a unicorn. They are the result of purposeful cultivation by folks like you and me. Did you have a supportive school culture? Adults worked to create that. Did you have an after-school activity that shaped you? Adults worked to build that. Did you learn how to handle conflict well? Adults taught and modeled that for you.

After studying this data, the president of the Search Institute, Peter Benson, concluded that "the experiences of young people do not fundamentally change unless individuals take personal responsibility to contribute to young people's healthy development."[4]

Those "individuals" he speaks of . . . that's us. You and me.

Parents Just Don't Understand
(Their Importance)

Parents have the greatest amount of potential impact in developing, facilitating, and cultivating assets in a teen's life. So when the YMCA study says that kids instinctively want more time with their parents, they're echoing this truth. They know they need something from their parents. They might not be able to articulate what it is, but they know they need it.

That roller coaster is scary, and the lap bar keeps them safe. This they understand.

And adults are right, too. There are scary, self-destructive choices that could derail or destroy a teen's potential. They just don't realize that the best preventive solution for that behavior happens to be themselves.

So how are we as parents doing? Well, in general, parents spend less time with their children as they enter their teenage years.[5] Dads spend an average of about twenty-six minutes per day one-on-one with their kids when the kids are younger than twelve, but that number drops to less than nine minutes per day during the teenage years. The average amount of time that a mom spends with her kids when they're young is about thirty-one minutes per day, but that number drops to about eleven minutes once the kids are teenagers.

I get it: When a teenager (or anyone, for that matter) is driving you crazy, the last thing you want to do is spend time with them. But what if their pushing and prodding and testing is actually a sign that they *need* you more than their maturity can articulate? What if they're scared and acting out?

What if the teenage years are a roller coaster and you're the lap bar? And what if following our knee-jerk reaction to withdraw isn't the right one?

To summarize:

> *Kids get about 57 minutes per day*
> *with Mom and Dad combined*

vs

> *Teens get about 20 minutes per day*
> *with Mom and Dad combined*

So as adults, we are spending almost two-thirds less time with teens at exactly the moment when they need more time with us.

When teens are brutally honest, they will tell you that what they secretly want most is more time with their dad and their mom. And you likely know—instinctively—that it's true.

Your teen needs your time.

What This Means for You

You've probably heard the expression "You get out of it what you put in." Your seventh-grade basketball coach probably said that. So did your high school English teacher. The same is true when it comes to trying to have an impact on your teen's life; your focused attention and time matters.

Quality time happens during quantity time. If you want your relationship with your teen to improve in quality, then you have to improve the quantity of time you're investing.

Unfortunately, there are NO SHORTCUTS to this.

Anyone who says there is a shortcut is likely trying to sell you something. You can't plan special, amazing moments to happen at exactly 7:23 P.M. They just happen.

The Power of Showing Up

After working with teenagers for the better part of two decades, I've learned that teenagers are a conundrum. They operate in one-word replies. They can be moody. They can be standoffish.

One of the best articulations of what it means to be a teenager is found in J. D. Salinger's famous novel *The Catcher in the Rye*, in the main character of Holden Caulfield. It's a touching story because Holden wants to do so much and yet can't do anything. He says again and again that he hates all phoniness, yet he frequently lies to other people. He desperately wants everyone to like him, but he's standoffish and completely self-absorbed. He wants to change the world, but he can't do anything. In other words, Holden Caulfield is a pretty accurate portrayal of a modern teenager. In fact, his character epitomizes the literary term "unreliable narrator."

Unreliable. That's the point. When you're a teenager, it seems like everything is unreliable. Everything is changing in your teen's life. And the problem with adolescence is that everyone is so terrified. Everyone knows that something big is happening to them—something that will change them and form them forever—but they don't have enough life experience to see through the frightening fog. So everyone is left terribly insecure and afraid.*

That's where you show up. I mean literally, you show up.

Consider what it means to a teenager who has an adult say to him or

---

* The Catholic theologians were right. There is a place between heaven and hell where people go to pay for their sins, and that place is called junior high.

her, "Hey, I care about you. I'm going to carve out this time for you." Showing up is a way of saying, "I'm here. Again. This is proof I care about you."

One of the most powerful things to teenagers is people proving they are devoted to them. In a social world filled with conditional love based on everything from performance to appearance to popularity, teens are truly craving someone to be interested in them. To care for them. To be there for them. To focus their time and attention on them.

Both the YMCA study and the Search Institute study share one common finding: Your teen wants and needs you. Despite the fact that sighs and eye-rolling are at an all-time high.

When I cited the research that most parents begin to pull away during the teenage years—both with their intentional time and focus—you likely did an internal audit. And if you're in the majority of adults I've interacted with, you probably realized that you've been doing exactly that.

It's time to reverse that trend. It's time to be intentional.

Some parents, when confronted with this reality, get defensive. "Who are you to say I'm not doing enough?"

Some parents, when confronted with this reality, rationalize their absence. "You don't understand how much pressure I'm under."

Some parents, when confronted with this reality, dive into shame. "I am a terrible person, and they are better off without me in their lives."

I know they're natural responses. I've done all three. But they're not helpful, are they?

If a water pipe burst in your house, it wouldn't help to pretend that having an in-home swimming pool could be fun. And you wouldn't say, "I'm a terrible homeowner. I should have known that pipe was about to break."

When a pipe breaks, you fix it.

Because you're the adult.

Teens Spell Trust T-I-M-E

If you're like most adults, you have underestimated how much your teen wants to spend time with you. But knowing that fact and actually spending quality time with your teen are two different things. Here are some steps you can take to create space in your schedule for intentionally connecting with your teen.

1. **Schedule one-on-one time.**

   If you want to prioritize your relationship with your teenager, then you need to make your teenager a true priority. You need to have time specifically set aside to bond with them. Pick a specific and certain time each month (example: the first Friday night of the month) and set aside that time for one-on-one time with your teen.

   Pro Tip: Fill in the hangout night on your calendar FIRST.

   Awhile back, I realized that if I waited until I had a whole week free to take a vacation, I would never take one. Life has a way of taking over your schedule. So now what I do is plan my family vacations FIRST. I mark them in pen on my calendar. And by "pen" I mean "red font" and by "calendar" I mean "Google Calendar." That week is totally off-limits to all other demands. Do the same with your teen hangout night. Examine your schedule and then set it up on your calendar.

2. **Do not cancel.**

   Don't let anything interrupt this night. Canceling is worse than never doing it at all. If you have a hard time saying no to other people, simply tell them, "I'm sorry, I have an appointment at that time," or, "I'm sorry, I have an important meeting then." You do have an important meeting/appointment. It's not a lie. Do not cancel.

Pro Tip: Seriously. Do not cancel.

Just making sure you read number two. Unless someone dies or you have a broken femur or two and are actually in the hospital, don't even think about canceling on your teenager. I'm telling you, you'll unravel their trust.

3. **Make it fun.**

Don't spend the night talking about how to make your relationship better with your teen. This hardly ever works. Instead, just spend the time doing something you both enjoy. In doing so, you're actually making the relationship better. Make a list of things you'd really enjoy doing, and then have your teenager do the same thing. Broadway musicals, local sporting events, day trips to interesting places, cool or fun restaurants they love—whatever. Compare lists, and then plan to do these activities during your scheduled time together.

Pro Tip: Take care of the details.

You're the adult. Be proactive and buy the tickets, or do whatever needs to be done.

4. **Expect it to be difficult.**

This is going to require all of your maturity because your teenager will likely push your buttons. No good and important things in life are accomplished without effort or resistance. The only things in life that just naturally happen without any human effort or resistance are mold, weeds, and weight gain. So expect there will be a wall to push through. Your teen might be disrespectful or aloof or distant or monosyllabic. Congrats! You have a teenager. Push through. Trust that this time together is sowing seeds. Practice it. You'll get better, just as you do with anything else. Don't be discouraged. If you feel like nothing happened, then great!

Pro Tip: Train, don't try.

If I asked you right now to go run a marathon, the chances of you being able to do that are pretty slim (unless you're an elite endurance athlete). Now, what if I told you that it was really, really important that you run the marathon? Would that help you complete it? Now, what if I encouraged you to "give it all you had" and to "try really, really hard." Would that help you complete all 26.2 miles? No. Because you don't *try* to run a marathon, you *train* for it. Each month is a chance to get better and build your relationship with your teen. These are training steps. So take the next step. And start training.

You Have Two Options

I've worked with parents and teens in some incredibly destructive situations that seemed hopeless. Here's what I have seen: Parents who intentionally make their teenager a priority—who focus both their time and their attention on their teen—always see a tangible return on that investment.

I'm not promising that things will be perfect. But they can get better.

One of the things that haunts parents the most is the nagging sense that they could have done more. Regret is a powerful thing. By focusing your time and attention on your teen, you'll be able to sit alone with your thoughts and give an honest assessment: "I gave it my best."

I'm not sure what the outcome will be. I don't have psychic powers or a 1985 DeLorean. But I do know that you have two options:

1. Do your best to be intentional, or
2. Slowly pull away and admit defeat.

I don't think number two is an option. And I don't think you do, either.

Your teenager is worth your time. But it can be difficult, mainly because there is no immediate feedback that what you're doing is even making a difference. Sometimes it even feels as though no one notices. This isn't true, but it can *feel* true.

No one gives out awards for what you're doing. Being a lap bar on a roller coaster is sort of a thankless job, isn't it? But of all the parts on that giant, complex roller coaster, when it comes to the well-being of actual humans, that lap bar is the most important.

Be the bar.

> *As is true with the lap bar on a roller coaster, teenagers will test you to see if you will hold.*

THE GAME HAS CHANGED AND SO MUST YOU

> We don't rise to the level of our expectations, we fall to the level of our training.
>
> —ARCHILOCHUS

> If you want to capture someone's attention, start off by quoting a dead Greek poet.
>
> —JOSH SHIPP

When I was a kid, one of my favorite reruns was a show called *Gilligan's Island*. The show followed a group of seven tourists who set sail from a tropic port, ran into a hurricane, and wound up stranded on a desert island. What made the show intriguing was how completely different each of the seven castaways were.

- There was the brilliant professor who could make a working radio from coconuts and spare wire, yet couldn't repair the small hole in the ship.
- There was the captain who was prone to hitting people with his hat when frustrated and who used the word "buddy" more often than anyone in human history.

- There were Ginger Grant and Mary Ann Summers, who caused endless debates among males across the planet about who represented a more perfect vision of idealized beauty.*
- There was the good-hearted but dim-witted first mate, Gilligan, after whom, inexplicably, the island was named.

But the two most fascinating characters to me were Thurston Howell III and his wife, Eunice, billionaires who suddenly found themselves out-of-sorts. These two were comic fodder for the show because the entire time they were marooned on the island, they attempted to keep up the facade of their lavish, luxurious lifestyle. And the audience laughed, because the Howells didn't realize the entire game had changed. This is the comedy of the Howells. Even though everything around them has changed, they don't want things to have changed. So they live in denial.

Now, here's the thing. I think a lot of us can relate to Thurston Howell III and Eunice. Many parents feel that at some point the game changed on them, and they liked the old game better. You wake up one day and feel as though, practically overnight, your sweet, innocent, simple child turned into a very complex, completely different, and at times utterly baffling teenager.

On Tuesday, you went to bed, and when you arose on Wednesday, the game had completely changed. You were traveling on a nice boat one moment, and then stranded on a desert island the next.

There's a reason we feel this way. It's because in many ways it's true.

---

* I don't want to get too much further into this, because this debate could turn unnecessarily divisive, but let me say this: I married a theater major from UCLA, so clearly I'm Team Ginger.

The One Shift You Must Make

As children become teenagers, their physical, cognitive, emotional, and social worlds dramatically change. And what teens need from parents shifts, too.

Many of life's major transitions demand fast-paced, nearly immediate changes that you don't ever really feel ready to handle. All parents remember the moment they brought home their first child from the hospital. The home that used to be just for a couple now had a brand-new life in it. It seemed like everything was different, quite literally overnight.

The same is true here, as kids go from children to teenagers. The game has changed. And if you don't change with it, you won't be effective.

So what do you do? I'm glad you asked.

YOUR OLD ROLE:
Air Traffic Controller

When kids are young, because of the fragile nature of their bodies and their nearly complete dependence, adults must be proactive in providing both protection and nurturing environments. This is the air traffic controller phase. When dealing with little kids, you have to be like an air traffic controller. You control what they eat. Where they go. Who they play with. When they go to bed. What they put in their noses. Because, like air traffic control, if you don't do your job, someone could get hurt. You need to be vigilant and thoughtful about nearly every aspect of your kid's life. And more than that, you know that if you didn't do so, it would be irresponsible.

WHAT THEY NEEDED:
Protection and nurturing environments

WHAT THEY WERE:
Nearly completely dependent

WHAT YOU DID:
Controlled nearly every detail of their life

YOUR DESIRED OUTCOME:
Safety and growth

YOUR NEW ROLE:
Coach

The role of air traffic controller is fantastic, but eventually it stops being effective. Those strategies are great for a while, and then suddenly they're not. They expire. Like milk. Unless you're lactose intolerant. In which case they will always make you feel bloated. (I think I've lost control of this metaphor.)

Imagine a young adult who is about to drive off to college. As the college student approaches the vehicle, the parent lifts his or her fully grown child into the car, reaches in, and fastens the young adult's seat belt. That'd be weird, right?

Why? Because they are in a different phase. Once kids hit the teenage years, what they need from parents dramatically changes. This can seem unfair, because the very same methods that once were highly effective are now frustratingly ineffective.

If you continue to try to control your teen as you did in the air traffic controller phase, it will backfire. Which is too bad, because you've spent the past decade perfecting the role. You're good at it, yes, but it's not what your teen needs.

When it comes to your teen, you can have control or you can have growth. But you can't have both.

Think about this: In just a few years you're going to be sending them out of the house. They are going to face some really difficult things. They'll need the confidence that comes from knowing they are competent at handling their own business. Adopting the coach mindset allows you to give your teen real-world practice for these challenges while you're still there to provide guidance and encouragement.

The game has changed. And so must you.

WHAT THEY NEED NOW:
Skills and practice navigating through the difficulties of life

WHAT THEY ARE NOW:
Half freedom seeker, half scared kid

WHAT YOU NEED TO DO NOW:
Prepare them to thrive without you

YOUR DESIRED OUTCOME:
Self-governance and growth

What Is a Coach?

Before we go any further we should address the caricatures that might come to mind when you read the word "coach." This is not a flush-faced individual who's throwing chairs and yelling at the ref; it's a caring adult who trains, prepares, pushes, and encourages his or her athletes to become more than they thought they could be.

I played baseball as a kid, and many of the greatest life lessons I learned were taught to me by coaches.

Let's review the characteristics of an effective coach.

Fact: A coach has clear authority.

One concern you might have is that this shift from air traffic controller to coach will mean less authority. But let's be clear: You're not giving up one ounce of your authority as a parent. It's how you'll exercise your authority that has shifted.

When your teen was four years old, think about how many levers of authority you had at your disposal. You had control of her calendar, her friends, her whereabouts—even her bedtime.

Now that she is fourteen years old, those levers of authority have mostly vanished, and you have to utilize new levers. Sure, you still control money, transportation, and access to technology. But the most effective levers of authority have to do with things like trust. Influence. Written, agreed-upon rules. And communication of values.

The best parents and caring adults feel a "burden of responsibility" regarding this authority. They understand it's a sacred position of trust, and they take that seriously.

Fact: A coach really matters and affects the outcome.

There's a reason that top sports organizations pay a premium for quality coaches. For example, since 1985, four teams in the NCAA men's basketball league have won an average of ten more NCAA tournament games than teams with identical seeding and records. So what made the difference? Their coaching. These teams were led by four of the most successful coaches in the history of the league, and because of these coaches, they won more tournament games than teams with comparable records.

Coaches provide tangible things, like making sure that players develop their skills, practices run smoothly, and morale is boosted through the ups and downs of a season. And those things are important. But coaches, especially great coaches, also bring intangible things—such as changing the emotional health in the culture of the organization, improving honest communication, and providing motivation. As complex humans, we're all motivated (and demotivated) by different things. Great coaches take the time to figure that out, and help everyone achieve more than they thought they could.

The Three Attributes of Great Coaches

So what makes a great coach a great coach? What key characteristics will help parents transition from effective air traffic controllers to effective coaches? Here are three attributes you must not only learn but embody.

ATTRIBUTE #1:
Focus on character development, not outcomes.

One of the key differences between great coaches and decent coaches is the emphasis on what is most important. Decent coaches stress that winning or outcomes are paramount. Great coaches rarely talk about outcomes because great coaches understand that you can't control outcomes. Things happen that are beyond your control: injuries, bad luck, or just a better opponent. You can't control outcomes, but you can control your preparation, your character, and how you handle both winning and losing. Great coaches know that life is far more than the achievements that may or may not come your way. It's about what's inside you.

GREAT COACH STORY

When Matt, a new teacher, was placed in a low-income, under-resourced, underperforming high school with twenty of his other colleagues, he realized there was a ton of work to do. Not only did Matt have to begin the arduous task of figuring out how to teach English, but he had to learn how to teach English well. The school's student population was testing poorly. With most students performing at least a grade or two below grade level in English, Matt knew that he'd have to move his students up 1.5 grade levels in a single year if his students were going to catch up. In addition to that, the diverse campus was still reeling from a racially motivated murder, which had resulted in incredible student trauma, massive teacher turnover, and an almost complete overhaul of the administration. It was a mess.

In his second year of teaching, the new principal named Matt the Advanced Placement English teacher. Matt then did something extraordinary. In this low-performing, under-resourced school, Matt began recruiting his junior students who showed promise, encouraging them to take AP English their senior year. He talked to his colleagues about which juniors they had who showed academic promise, and recruited those students as well. Nearly everyone pushed back, including his colleagues. "Don't you know how tough that AP English test is? It's the equivalent of passing sophomore college English." The students pushed back. "I can't pass that test." Their parents pushed back. "Wouldn't it be better if my teen were in a class more his or her . . . speed?" Matt pushed back harder. And based largely on the size of his personality, he convinced fifty-eight students to sign up for AP English in their senior year. Enough for two whole classes of AP English.

For the next year, Matt* taught AP English to fifty-eight students. In May, all of them took the test. The test is scored on a scale of 1–5, with a score of 3 or higher being passing. Scores of 4 or 5 all but guarantee college credit. Of Matt's fifty-eight students, only ten passed.

That's a 17 percent pass rate.

Matt came under fire from everyone, it seemed. Even the district office, which didn't like the way those numbers looked. "Why

---

* I would be remiss not to mention that Matt had an incredible principal who assigned him a mentor teacher and even contacted a supremely gifted retired English master teacher who came out of retirement to help Matt. Both of these older educators saw what Matt was trying to do and met with him weekly to help him be a better teacher.

don't we have just one smaller class of AP English offered next year?" they said. "This kind of failure rate doesn't look good."

Matt, as was his custom, pushed back.

"Failure? Failure! Do you know why my students didn't pass the AP English test this year?" he asked. "They didn't pass because of my fifty-eight students, thirty-five spoke a language other than English in their home growing up. They are nonnative English speakers. And section 2 of the free response section featured a poem by William Blake written in 1794. In 1794! The English language from that period was too archaic for my nonnative speakers to access because the English language has changed so much.

"But on section 1 and 3, which featured modern poems from modern poets, they passed. Here's the data. They passed. Which means that last year, we had a grand total of zero students in AP English, and this year we had fifty-eight students, all of whom, at one point during this test, received a passing grade on a college-level essay they wrote analyzing a poem or piece of prose.

"I had fifty-eight students staying late after school, working in teams to pull apart poetry from Frost and Dickinson and Langston Hughes. I had fifty-eight students who read five classic novels this year, and understood all five. I had fifty-eight students who volunteered to not take the easy road their senior year, and push themselves toward college-level academics instead. And I had fifty-eight kids who all pushed their minds to learn. That's not failure. That's a rousing success. And next year I want room in the schedule for three classes of AP English, because I'm going to need it."

Matt would get what he wanted. He would successfully lobby for his school and his district to make a broader push to increase the number of AP classes offered, and the number of students recruited to take AP courses. His pass rate went up a bit in the coming years, but not a lot. But that didn't matter to Matt.

Every year, at graduation, the senior class chooses Matt as one of the four teachers given the honor of escorting the graduates to the platform during the ceremony. Because that 17 percent pass rate isn't the outcome he was going for. Matt was never focused on the outcomes. He was focused on helping his students see that hard work, teamwork, dedication to their own education, responsibility, problem-solving, and perseverance in the face of a big, difficult task were more important than the numerical grade.

And that's a lesson those students will never forget.

ATTRIBUTE #2:
Intentionally discuss "game-over" failures.

Game-over failures are failures that will substantially derail a person's life. They will dramatically hurt a person's potential. Game-over failures are life situations that, if you enter into them, will destroy your chances for success (or seriously hinder them to the point where they're very statistically improbable). And great coaches talk about these game-over failures because they are a legitimate and tragic danger to their players.

There is a reason that parents of teens sometimes freak out. It's because teenagers have the ability to make choices that can result in a game-over failure.

A few years ago, the National Center for Policy Analysis did a study of the thirty-one million Americans who, according to the latest US Census data, live in households with incomes below the poverty level.[6] One policy adviser sifted through the data and found that a person from these circumstances has more than an 80 percent chance of avoiding crippling long-term poverty if he or she does three things:

1. Graduates from high school.
2. Waits until at least twenty-one years of age to get married.
3. Waits to have children until after marriage.

If a person does not follow even *one* of those three things, that number flips and the person now has nearly an 80 percent chance of living in long-term poverty.

My point is not that monetary hardship is an unrecoverable challenge. It's that monetary hardship is really difficult, and we know from studies that it's incredibly limiting to human flourishing. If it's possible to set teens up for success, we'd like them to know the best path—and that means discussing what could keep them from that path.

Think about that teen you care about. What are some game-over failures that you want to see them avoid at all costs? Perhaps teen pregnancy. Drug abuse. Driving while under the influence. Blowing off their own education. Having friends who are terrible influences. You must begin talking about these things with your teen, openly and honestly.

GREAT COACH STORY

Vivian is a high school biology teacher, and every year, on the Friday before prom, she stops all her classes twenty minutes early for a very particular lesson plan. Vivian projects onto the whiteboard a picture of herself at her senior prom. The kids get a kick out of Vivian's hair and how young she looks. They make jokes about what it was like living among the dinosaurs. And then Vivian shows a picture of a gnarled old oak tree, big and thick, about eight feet off to the side of what looks like a winding country road. Vivian then tells her students—all of whom are juniors and seniors—why that tree matters to her.

You see, when Vivian was a junior in high school, she got asked to the prom by a young man named Noah. Noah had somehow managed to get permission to borrow his father's car to drive Vivian and their friends to prom. And this was no ordinary car. It was a 1956 Chevy Bel Air convertible, candy-apple red, with a

1978 Chevy Corvette V8 430 hp engine under the hood. It was a beautiful car.

Noah picked up Vivian in this car, along with two of their other friends. They had a great night, and after Noah dropped Vivian and her friend off, he drove out to the back roads. He wanted to open up the throttle and see what the car could do. He sped along those roads at a dizzying speed, toward a bump in the road where Noah hoped he might even be able to get some air. He hit that small hill in the road going more than 70 mph. But then he lost control and crashed into the old oak tree. The sudden impact of going from 70 mph to 0 mph caused Noah's seat belt to slice through him like a wire. The paramedics pronounced him dead on the scene.

Vivian still tears up when she tells the story of Noah, and the tragic loss of a bright life ended far too soon. But her students get the message, loud and clear. Drive safely. Don't drive under the influence. Don't get into a car with anyone who has. Don't be macho. Don't drag-race. Don't show off. Because it could be a game-over failure. Vivian has hundreds of lesson plans each year, but this is the one every student remembers. And it's largely because she has the honesty and vulnerability to discuss game-over failures with her students, and the students know she does it because she cares about them.

ATTRIBUTE #3:
Discipline from values, not from emotion.

When you think about great coaches, a couple probably come to mind who have hot tempers. Maybe you can imagine them yelling at the referee or the umpire. Or yelling at their players. Or breaking a clipboard over their knee. Or, if you're from Indiana, throwing a chair across the floor.

But although negative emotional outbursts are a part of being human, they also have the potential to be distracting and dangerous to players.

When a teenager does something wrong, rebellious, or confrontational, there's often something inside us that makes us want to react in anger. But as I've discovered myself, this hardly ever helps the situation.

Some adults flip out with aggressive, emotional outbursts. The strange thing is, adults often do this in an attempt to regain control of the situation, but more often than not, negative emotional outbursts cause people to lose respect for you.

Conversely, some grown-ups do the opposite. Instead of flipping out, they "flip in." The emotions are so strong, some adults shut down emotionally. Some people call this "giving someone the cold shoulder" or "stonewalling" or "the silent treatment." Regardless of the name, the outcome is the same: It's a relational withdrawal from the situation. In some ways, this can be more dangerous because it's all internal. There are no clearly observable clues given to friends and family that something is wrong and that you need support.

Regardless of your tendency, the results are the same: You're governed by your emotions. But when you are working with teens, you must remember who the adult is and who needs to be acting like the more mature party. Rather than having an emotional reaction, react based on principles of value.

The name of the game with discipline is to establish agreed-upon expectations and then outline clear privileges and consequences. Negative emotional outbursts (flipping out *or* flipping in) almost never work as legitimate consequences. If you do the hard work beforehand to establish clear values* that everyone can agree upon, along with clear rewards and costs, and then have the guts to stick to them, it can help you keep your cool. And keeping control of your emotions can help you keep control of the situation.

---

* I'll walk you through how to do this in Part 3.

GREAT COACH STORY

When the 1972 NCAA men's basketball season was over, UCLA star center Bill Walton—one of the best college basketball players of all time—decided to express himself. After a summer of fun touring with the Grateful Dead and going backpacking on the John Muir Trail in the Sierras, Walton came back to practice with a thick red Afro and a beard that would make a lumberjack (or Gimli) proud. Which all sounds fine until you realize that his coach, John Wooden, had a strict no-facial-hair policy for his athletes and didn't allow haircuts to be longer than two inches.

Wooden frowned. "What's this?" he said as he tugged on Walton's beard. "This won't do." Walton could not believe it. He went into Coach Wooden's office and laid out his case. Walton had just lead UCLA to an undefeated season and a national title, and had won player of the year. Coach Wooden was being unreasonable. He didn't have the right to tell players how to personally express themselves.

"It sounds like this is very important to you, this personal expression with your hair," Wooden said.

"It is," said Walton.

"And you're right. I don't have the right to tell players to wear shorter hair or not wear shorter hair."

"Good," Walton said.

"But I do have the right to determine who's going to play," Wooden said. "And we're sure going to miss you."

After Walton realized that Wooden wasn't kidding, he hopped on his bike and rode as fast as he could to a local barbershop, where he commanded them to shave off all his hair, while he sat in the chair and shaved his own beard off with a plastic disposable razor. He got to practice about five minutes late, but Wooden didn't discipline him. That season, UCLA would go undefeated 30-0 again, but the lesson Wooden taught—that all discipline flows out of clear, established values—never left Walton.

What Do Great Coaches Do?

Let's get practical. We've talked about what a coach is, and what attributes great coaches have, but now we need to talk about what great coaches do. What does it mean to be an effective parent who operates as a coach in a teen's life?

PREGAME = REHEARSE

The key question: *What potential challenges do teens need to be prepared to face?*

One of the responsibilities of a coach is to help simulate real-world environments, minus the stress and fear. That's what practice is. And to be an effective coach for a teen, you have to run some practices. The general rule of thumb is to ask yourself what particular situations your teenager may face, and if there is anything that you can do to help prepare them to face that specific issue.

It helps when I ask myself the following question: "What is the [realistic] worst-case scenario my teen is going to face in this situation?" And then I follow with the mantra "Expect the best, but prepare for the worst."

For example, my friend's twelve-year-old son recently went on a class trip to a local amusement park, and part of this friend's preparation was to sit down with his son and outline all the (realistic) worst-case scenarios.

They made it into a game. He had his son go into his room and then come back into the living room with everything he thought he might need for the day at the amusement park. Everything. His son emerged from his room, confident he'd remembered everything. They then ran through every (realistic) worst-case scenario:

DAD: You lose your wallet, what would you do?

SON: Tell my leader and ask him for help. Explain to him that you'll pay him back.

DAD: Smart.

SON: Or borrow money from Josiah. His parents always give him extra money.

DAD: You get separated from your group and can't find anyone, what would you do?

SON: Uh, call my leader.

DAD: But do you know your leader's cell phone number?

SON: No, but I will ask him for it at the front gate and put it in my cell phone.

DAD: It's super hot out, and you're very thirsty. You need water. What would you do?

SON: They have water fountains. And food courts.

DAD: How is a food court going to help you?

SON: I can fill up my water bottle at the soda machines with water AND get free ice.

DAD: You don't know what time it is, and you have to meet your group at three P.M. What would you do?

SON: Dad, everyone has a cell phone. I'll just ask someone what time it is.

DAD: You forgot to wear deodorant. You smell like a decaying skunk. You're standing in line next to Ashley and you think she's cute. What's your game plan?

SON: Dad! Gross.

DAD: Okay, we'll deal with that problem later.

They talked through all the potential scenarios and brainstormed together what to do in a very low-stress environment. My buddy's son was even cracking jokes, saying that if he got lost, "I know what to do, Dad. I'll just fire off a flare." In the end, his son logged the cell number of his adult leader, brought an insulated water bottle with him, and tucked his wallet into his small backpack. He was ready and confident for anything. Luckily, nothing even remotely bad happened and the trip was an amazing experience for him. But if something had gone wrong, my buddy was sure his son would know what to do. Preparing his son in advance for the real challenges he could face gave them both confidence.

Prepare for the worst, but expect the best.

POSTGAME = REVIEW

The key question: *What did we learn?*

The evaluation phase is crucial when dealing with teenagers. And the central question you must ask is "What did we learn from this?"

Let's go back to the example with my friend's son going to the amusement park. At five P.M., when my buddy picked up his son from the park, they talked about how the day went. During that time, my buddy was asking all sorts of questions. What was your favorite part of the day? What was the most fun? Was there anything that was stressful during the day? Did anything not go as planned? What went well? What didn't go well? As his son was talking, my buddy was doing two things:

1. Listening.
2. Making mental notes about what needed to be rehearsed in the future.

Your teen's responses are the equivalent of reviewing game film. If a player misses a key free throw at the end of the game, as the coach in charge, your response should be "I need to better prepare them for free throws." And then you make adjustments.

Here's a handy postgame review checklist:
- What worked?
- What didn't?
- How could you improve?
- How can I support you?

For example, my buddy had the following conversation with his son:

DAD: Was there anything that was stressful during the day?
SON: Well, there was one thing.
DAD: What was it?
SON: Well, we were in this big group, and the first rides we rode were awesome, but then they wanted to go on the Vortex, which has corkscrews. And I'd never been on a corkscrew. So I kind of didn't want to go.
DAD: Did you say anything?
SON: No, I didn't want to say anything or not ride it because I didn't want everyone to think I was a wimp.
DAD: So what did you do?
SON: I just rode it.

My buddy (correctly) saw that there was a potential issue here. Here was something that his son didn't really want to do, but he didn't feel comfortable speaking up for himself. Was it because of peer pressure? Was it because he didn't want to disappoint people? Did he feel out-numbered? What was going on? As a parent, you're making note of that. Because right now the stakes are rides in the amusement park. But if your teen doesn't develop the ability to speak up for himself, the stakes will inevitably be raised in the future. There will be pressure to cheat on that test. There will be a drug passed around.

There will be a situation where he'll need to speak up for himself.

My buddy realized that before a real issue arose, he needed to focus more on giving his son opportunities to speak up for himself. So he began to make minor changes to help him practice that skill. When the family was going out to eat, he was sure to give ample room for his son to articulate his own preference. They were able to discuss where to go, and his son was able to speak up and express himself. And at the annual physical with their family doctor, my buddy coached his son on how to talk to the doctor himself and ask any questions he had. Through changes like these, he began teaching his son that he was encouraged and empowered to talk to people in authority, to ask questions, and to speak up about things that were important to him.

And my buddy achieved all of this with his son because he did an evaluation, paid attention, and then made minor adjustments.

DURING THE GAME = RELEASE

The key question: *Are they ready to succeed without me?*

There's a reason this section is here, after pregame and postgame, instead of being placed chronologically. Because unlike, say, a soccer coach, the game of a teen's life doesn't unfold on a manicured field right in front of you, and you don't have a whistle to call time out and make adjustments. Really, for most of the life situations you're preparing your teen for, you will not be around. They will have to do this on their own. In most real-world situations, there's not a whole lot you can do. It's out of your hands. If you want to influence the outcome, you're going to have to do the work during the pregame.

Why Make the Shift to Coaching?

The fact of the matter is that for many parents, making the mental shift from air traffic controller to coach can be extremely frightening. As teens become more and more autonomous and independent, the results and outcomes can seem as though they are increasingly out of your hands. But they are not. The switch to becoming a coach will set you up for the best shot at real influence and, more important, will truly help your teen.

But this is a very difficult process. It will require work. It will require you to let go of certain ways of thinking, and it will cause you to build proficiency in something that's very tough to do. So why would you do this? Why would any adult go through the trouble of making these kind of strategic shifts?

Here's why:

On April 2, 1912, the RMS *Titanic*, the largest ocean liner ever built in the history of mankind, was put out in open ocean to undergo sea trials to measure the vessel's performance and general seaworthiness.

After the trial, the inspectors and engineers said there were two warning signs:

- Of the more than three million rivets holding the ship together, inspectors found that the rivets at the front of the ship were made from iron and slag instead of the much harder steel rivets used elsewhere on the ship. The inspectors worried that this substandard iron would make the bow of the ship considerably weaker.

- During the trial, a fire developed in the coal stored in the starboard side coal bunker. It was not fully extinguished until a few days later. The inspectors and engineers were worried that the fire may have made the hull plates in this area more brittle.

In the rush to get this ship out to sea (and to start making money), these concerns were wholly ignored. As you know, the *Titanic* hit an iceberg going almost 23 miles per hour, hitting the hull plates on the starboard side that had been made more brittle by the fire. The weaker iron rivets in the bow popped, opening seams in the hull and hurrying the ship's demise. It's no accident that the flooding stopped at the point in the hull where the steel rivets began.

The point is this: If you don't coach your teen—if you don't run through pregame rehearsals or stop and evaluate performances—then you won't notice when warning signs pop up. And if you don't pay attention to warning signs and make the necessary corrections, bad things can happen.

You can't predict every iceberg, but you can make the ship stronger.

What to Do When Your Teen Fails

When your teen fails (and your teen will fail), you have to do the hard work of figuring out what's going on—whether we're talking about failing a chemistry test, plowing into the neighbor's mailbox, or coming home drunk from a party. Here's what happens if you sit down with your teen and ask the question, "What did we learn from this?"

- The use of the word "we" implies support, showing that you're both in this together. For better or worse. This is disarming because after every failure, teens are afraid of being singled out and punished. There will likely be consequences to their actions, but your first overture must be to send the message that you're in a partnership. As Dr. Jane Nelsen, coauthor of the Positive Discipline series, says, "Connection before correction." **This is critical because it allows your teen to get out of fight-or-flight mode and learn.**

- It puts the emphasis on the fact that learning is part of failure and life, and that's normal. This is both healthy and true.

- It shifts the focus from the immediately felt failure that just happened (the past) to the growth needed to be successful later (the future). This is more helpful because we can't (yet!) go back in time and change the past.

- It helps you and your teen identify what went well and why. This gives you and your teen insight into his or her unique strengths.

- It helps you and your teen identify what went poorly and why. This gives you and your teen insight into his or her unique weaknesses.

- It will help you more easily identify the simulations and practices now necessary to improve the outcomes that didn't go as well as you planned.

If you're a coach, you're going to have to deal with losses. But being a great coach means that how you handle losses matters. And how you handle losing isn't just about you—it's about teaching your teen how they should handle these losses as well. As the adult, you have access to two crucial things your teen doesn't:

1. **Perspective.** Your teen doesn't know how big or small a deal this is, so don't overreact. Choose your words very carefully, and be accurate and thoughtful in your diagnosis about why the failure happened—and what that means in the grand scheme of things.
2. **Encouragement.** The biggest gifts a coach can give players are motivation and encouragement. It's like air to them—and during this time, they're going to need the oxygen. As Dr. Martin Luther King Jr. once said, "The true measure of a man is not how he behaves in moments of comfort and convenience, but how he stands at times of controversy and challenges."

Help your teen keep these things in mind in the face of their losses, and you'll be fulfilling your duty as a great coach in the game of life.

> *You can have control. Or you can have growth.*
> *But you can't have both.*

YOU'LL WANT AND NEED HELP

first saw the game televised on ESPN, and I was captivated. This was not a simple game of chance. It was a mental game where you could eviscerate your opponent using psychological craftiness. And the players: These were glamorous athletes, competing with tens of thousands of dollars on the line.

I'm talking, of course, about Texas Hold'em.

I wanted to be part of the action, so I decided to play online. I learned the lingo: The final table. The bad beat. The river. The flux capacitor. The nifty banjo.

Okay, those last two were made up.

Turns out, I am fairly good at poker. I started winning money. Not only am I hypercompetitive, but I'm drawn to strategic games like poker. I loved the rush.

However, like any other addiction, this one became sneakily destructive. Online poker began to slowly consume me. I would go to sleep thinking about how I should have played hands differently. How I could have won.

It became the white-hot center of my thoughts and life, and it began to isolate me. I would lock myself in my office and play four or five hours a day, pretending to be working. I didn't make time for family or friends, and when I did, I fantasized about returning to play a few hands.

One day my good friend Jason came over to our house to share some news with me. After months of trying, he and his wife were pregnant with their first child.

And as Jason stood there in the doorway of my office, telling me this glorious news, I sat behind my laptop . . . in the middle of a poker hand. I didn't get up. I didn't shake his hand. I didn't make extended eye contact. I didn't hug him. I didn't congratulate him.

Nothing.

The sound of the front door closing downstairs jarred me out of my haze. I realized what I had just done, and the full weight and reality of how this addiction to online gambling was impacting my life came crashing down on me.

But it was more than that. Ever since I was a little foster kid, I hated the utter lack of control I had in many areas of my life. I hated that things were never permanently mine, that I was constantly being moved from house to house, that people would enter my life and then leave. So I had worked tirelessly to make sure that if something in my life could be controlled, I would control it. I wanted to control life so that it couldn't hurt or disappoint me (impossible, but you can see how I got there). I remember nearly collapsing onto the floor as I realized that this online poker and gambling thing had me. It was in control, not me. And worst of all, I didn't know if I could break free from its web.

A wave of emotions came over me. Fear. Disgust. Shame.

My wife found me, sobbing, on my knees.

Like many of us, although I appeared to have my act together, deep down, I was a flawed human being.

Traps in My Own Backyard

On the day of my epiphany about Texas Hold'em, I realized I'd fallen into a trap. It had been camouflaged and hidden from plain sight. I had not meant to stumble into it. After all, nobody says, "You know what I'm going to do today? I'm going to become slowly addicted to online gambling and isolate myself from the most important relationships in my life and hurt myself and whole lot of other people." No one means to do that. But that's what a trap is.

And if you don't keep your eyes open and look where you're walking and know what to look for (woven grass mats!) and stay intentional, any of us can fall into a trap.

But what bothered me the most was that the trap didn't seem to be something external. There wasn't someone out there who was trying to capture me with nefarious means. This trap—and others like it— seemed to be coming from inside of me.

This trap had to do with my character, the way I thought about things, the way I processed things. This trap had to do with my background and how I had been raised. This trap seemed to bubble out of . . . me. And it was a blind spot. I truly didn't see it until I found myself at the bottom of the pit.

After the online gambling episode, I couldn't help but think the following:

- I am afraid that I will fall into a trap.
- I am afraid that my inadequacies will end up hurting my kids.
- I am not strong enough to prevent my character defects from harming those I love.

This bothered me deeply, but there was no pretending anymore. I understood that if I was not careful, I could easily fall into a trap. I could wind up doing unintentional damage to the people I care about the most.

All of us come to the table with our own issues, and how we deal with those issues really matters.

Who you are as a person directly affects your kids, and it directly affects your ability to be a good parent. We need help with our own issues, in order to be better for the teens around us.

Because, after all, apples don't fall far from trees.

It makes me think of what a mentor of mine, Ken Van Meter, once said: "Teens learn a little bit from what we say . . . a little bit more from what we do . . . but the most from who we are."

We need to be thoughtful about the type of person we are (and are becoming)—not just for our own sake, but for those who depend on us.

Let's Talk About Two H-Words

The ancient Greeks compiled and shared dozens of cautionary tales about this first H-word, to warn everyone about its dangers. Even today, some of our most beloved stories revolve around this word.

The word is "hubris."

Hubris is from the Greek language and it means excessive pride or self-confidence. Now, you might hear this and think, "Hey! What's wrong with self-confidence?" But hubris means you are *too* self-confident. There's a gap between inflated self-perception and a much more modest reality.

Hubris can manifest itself in many ways. In literature, it's often the dominant personality flaw that causes the tragic downfall of a character. This is one of the most prevailing themes in ancient Greek literature—Achilles, Odysseus, Arachne, Icarus, and Niobe all fall due to their hubris.

My favorite example of hubris comes from the classic film *Jurassic Park*, where a group of scientists create a park full of giant dinosaurs, believing that human ingenuity can prevent anything from going wrong. They wildly overestimate mankind's ability to control nature,*

---

* My favorite line from *Jurassic Park* is spoken by Jeff Goldblum's quirky mathematician character, Ian Malcolm, who says, "Your scientists were so preoccupied with whether or not they could that they didn't stop to think if they should."

which results in a lawyer cowering on a toilet and then getting eaten by a T. rex. Also, some bad things happen.

By now I know what you're thinking. "But, Josh, I'm not planning on using genetic modification to create apex alpha predators anytime soon. What does this have to do with me?"

Well, we all have a choice. And it's a rather binary choice.

We can choose hubris. Or we can choose the antidote to hubris, the exact opposite. Instead of a potentially tragic overestimation of yourself, this word represents a sober and accurate self-assessment.

That word is "humility."

That's our choice.

Now, there's a lot of confusion about the word "humility." Some people think it's pretending that you're not good at something when you actually are. But humility isn't pretending that something isn't true when it is. Humility means "a modest or accurate view of one's own self or importance." It's understanding that even though I'm good at some things, that doesn't make me better or more important than other people.

We've all met people who believe they are better than other people and that their existence, opinions, and preferences are more important than everyone else's.* Are they fun to be around? Do they make Thanksgiving more enjoyable? No. No, they do not.

Humility takes a tremendous amount of courage. Self-reflection is terrifying—it means taking accurate stock of who you are and who you are not. It means being brave enough to listen to (and not dismiss or get defensive of) lists of your weaknesses and shortcomings, as well as acknowledging your clear strengths without becoming puffed up.

Humility is a high-wire tightrope walk. But it's an important part of being a caring adult.

---

* Alternatively, just check out the comments sections on the Internet.

What This Means for Us

As parents and caring adults, we have a choice. In our unique role, we can choose hubris or humility. And whichever you and I choose, that decision will have a real impact on our teen.

Here's what our options look like.

OPTION A:
Hubris means living by a falsehood.

"I am finite and limited as a human, and that's not okay."

Because:
- I am not that flawed.
- I will just work harder.
- I will redouble my efforts.
- Mine is the only voice I will listen to.

Therefore: I can do this all by myself.

How this affects your teen: It establishes a household culture of fear and shame.

OPTION B:
Humility means living by a truth.

"I am finite and limited as a human, and that's okay."

Because:
- I have blind spots.
- I have weaknesses.

- I have frailties.
- I can be self-centered.

Therefore: I could use some help.

How this affects your teen: It establishes a household culture of trust and connection.

Choosing humility doesn't mean you're choosing defeat. It means you realize you want and need help. It means you don't want to get eaten by a T. rex. But it does not make you weak. Instead, it makes you brave.

Humility is the way to gain the trust and confidence of your teen.

The Four Major Parent Traps

There are four major traps that we fall into as parents and caring adults: the comfort trap, the approval trap, the control trap, and the performance trap.

Interestingly enough, these traps are often just a misuse of a strength, which makes sense because every positive character trait has a dark side. For example, detail-oriented people can, if they're not careful, turn that strength into an all-consuming obsession or perfectionism. Each strength has a downside when it is misused or taken to an extreme.

I've laid out details about the four major traps below, and I've provided comparative examples of real parents who have successfully dealt with these traps and who have succumbed to them. Although the names have been changed, these are real examples.

My goal here is twofold. First, I wanted to bring the manifestation of these traps into clear relief. While these cases are not normative, they should serve as sober warnings.

And second, I hope that seeing the honest and humble path taken by these parents will provide you with hope and a road map to a solid relationship with your teen.

It's possible that only one of the four traps will resonate with you. Please try to read about each of them with an open mind to see which one you personally drift toward. Simply understanding our own frailties as parents will help us perform this important role better.

PARENT TRAP #1: THE COMFORT TRAP

Never want to do anything hard or difficult. Afraid to try because of fear of failing.

THE FALSE NARRATIVE: "I'm in way over my head. I'm not cut out for this."

THE MODUS OPERANDI: Ignore and disengage.

THE UNINTENDED MESSAGE TO TEENS: "Adults aren't reliable" and "You are not worth my time and effort."

THE ANTIDOTE: Wade into areas of your own ignorance and fear for the sake of figuring out how to help.

THE HUBRIS CASE STUDY

When I met first met Frank and his wife, their daughter, Jamie, was involved in a very bad scene at junior high school. She was actively using various drugs, was cutting herself, and was sexually active with a twenty-year-old. All of this came as a complete surprise to Frank, who had been in the dark about everything. But that was largely because Frank didn't *want* to know. He was in a deep state of denial about Jamie's behavior.

Frank's wife had a son and a daughter from a previous marriage, and two years after they got married, she gave birth to Jamie. At first Frank liked being a dad. He found that babies were pretty easy, like his sweet-cheeked, compliant little girl. But teenagers? Not so much. The social dynamics, the attitudes, the confusing matrix of emotions. It required too much, so Frank began to disengage. He'd come home and plop in his recliner in front of the television. Frank wouldn't even eat at the table with the family. He'd take his plate and eat in the living room, in front of the TV. He started spending more time at work, coming home later and later.

Frank was unwilling to wade into Jamie's life. He would shrug his shoulders when I asked him what steps he could take to engage with his daughter. I would press him, and Frank would change the subject, as if even thinking about this problem was too much for him. And although Frank said that he loved Jamie (and I believed him), the deliberate actions he took to disengage from every aspect of his daughter's life screamed otherwise.

Jamie chose to get professional help. And her mother was an absolute champ, supporting and visiting her daughter and providing her with a level of emotional support and love that I've rarely seen. Frank did not. He withdrew even more.

As a result, Frank has a dysfunctional relationship with all three kids. When I asked Jamie if her father loved her, Jamie said, "Maybe. But I never felt it." When asked about their stepfather, the other two children (now grown) said that the best word to describe Frank's role in their life was "worthless."

THE HUMILITY CASE STUDY

Both of Michael's biological parents were crystal meth addicts. There were times when they crashed so hard, even the sounds of their own crying infant wouldn't wake them.

The authorities who investigated are still a bit unclear how Michael even survived. What's assuredly true is this: Michael wasn't held as a baby. He spent most of his infancy isolated and alone for weeks on end. His cries were all ignored. This had a devastating effect on Michael's development.

At the age of eight, Michael was sexually assaulted by a guest at his parents' home. The abuse continued, and eventually, Michael's parents began selling Michael for drug money. When the police were alerted to what was going on, they found Michael hiding like a feral animal in the back room. Michael had learned to hold in his bowels, and if someone got close enough, Michael would spray his feces like a skunk to repulse them.

The county psychologists diagnosed Michael with reactive attachment disorder, in which a child doesn't establish healthy attachments with parents or caregivers.

The State of California tracked down Michael's closest living relative—his uncle, Steven, who'd been estranged from his younger brother for nearly a decade. Steven was married to Joy, and they had no kids of their own and enjoyed the pace and comfort of their life. But when they heard what had been done to Michael, they couldn't stop weeping.

They decided to take Michael in.

I met with Steven as he and Joy were trying to process this decision. This was not Steven's biological child, and he had never been a parent before in his life. Let alone the parent of a preteen with severe emotional issues that at times baffled even clinical psychologists. This would completely upend his life and the balance of his days. But Steven and Joy dived in.

It took Steven and Joy seven years to break through to Michael—to begin to undo the damage from those first ten years of Michael's horrific life. But they did. For seven years they went to counseling four times a week. Twice for Michael as a family, once as a couple, and once individually. This was a herculean amount of work. But now Michael, who is seventeen, is doing a lot better. He loves baseball and is the starting second baseman for his high school team. He has a good sense of humor and good friends. And he has Steven and Joy, whom he calls Dad and Mom.

What changed in the equation of Michael's life? Steven and Joy, who although they were afraid, completely in over their heads, and wanted desperately to disengage, decided to push forward. They figured out how to help.

PARENT TRAP #2: THE APPROVAL TRAP

Need to be liked by everyone.

THE FALSE NARRATIVE: "If someone is upset with me, it means there's something wrong with me."

THE MODUS OPERANDI: Nonconfrontational. Doesn't set boundaries.

THE UNINTENDED MESSAGE TO TEENS: "I don't make the rules. Do whatever you want."

THE ANTIDOTE: Understand that love means setting clear boundaries and following through with consequences.

THE HUBRIS CASE STUDY

I'll never forget the first words that Bob said to me as he walked through the door, practically dragging his teenage son Aaron by his maroon hoodie along with him. "Would you tell him to listen to me?!"

I learned that Aaron was verbally abusive to his dad. He was yelling, screaming, slamming doors, destroying property around the house, and throwing massive tantrums, usually because he wasn't getting his way.

This wasn't surprising to me: Teens are emotional creatures and are prone to outbursts. There are times when simply asking them to empty the dishwasher is met with such strong resistance, it's like you asked them to clean all the bathrooms in Grand Central Station . . . with their tongue.

What was surprising was Bob's response. Bob would capitulate. If Aaron threw a tantrum about something he wanted, Bob would buy it for him on the spot. If Aaron asked to go to a party and Bob said no, Aaron would rant until his dad let him go.

The thing was, Bob was really a great guy. Super funny, the life of the party, an amazing storyteller, and liked by nearly everyone. And that was the problem. Bob was too well liked. He wanted to be liked so badly, he had unintentionally become a pushover.

I explained to Bob that boundaries exist to help teens understand the concept of authority, and to enable them to learn what behavior is clearly expected of them and what behavior is just plain wrong. If Bob continued to refuse to set boundaries, Aaron would have to learn about them the hard way.

Bob and I worked together to brainstorm behavior contracts, with clear and detailed consequences for Aaron if he broke the house rules. But as we were wrapping up, Bob said, "What am I going to do if he doesn't follow these rules?"

"Enforce the consequences we've talked about," I said. "Remember . . . you're the parent!"

Bob asked if I could be the one to enforce the consequences. "I think it will work better coming from you," he said.

But I knew what Bob meant. He meant, "I'm afraid Aaron will be mad at me, and if *you* punish him, he'll hate you and not me." And I also knew that as long as Bob thought and behaved that way, Aaron was going to be in real trouble.

THE HUMILITY CASE STUDY

I sat in Sabrina's living room with several other friends and family as part of an intervention to help her figure out what to do about her son, RJ.

RJ was a senior in high school, and he was headed down a destructive path. He was skipping school, taking money from his sisters, and hanging out with a crowd of former gang members. We sat around, trying to convince Sabrina that the greatest act of love she could provide for RJ was to enforce clear and immediate boundaries, even if that meant that her son would react in anger and perhaps not even talk to her. Even if it meant kicking her son, who was eighteen years old, out of her house if he chose to behave the way he was behaving.

Sabrina, a caring single mom, didn't know what to do.

"It's my son!" she said, crying. "I love him. I just can't do this. I can't kick him out."

And of course Sabrina did love RJ. Deeply. She saw through his failings and destructive behavior to the goodness she believed was still there.

People like Sabrina who are afraid of conflict are at their core peace-makers. And this is a great thing. But some things you simply cannot make peace with. You must confront them instead.

Sabrina needed to understand that love does not mean an endorsement of every single action a person takes. RJ needed to know that his choices were dangerous, and that if he chose to continue to behave in this manner, he was not welcome in Sabrina's home.

So Sabrina laid out her grievances with her son. She explained what she expected. She explained the consequences. And we were all there to listen and provide support for Sabrina. RJ was not happy. He stormed off, and as the screen door slammed, Sabrina let out a cry.

"I think my heart just broke," she said.

But RJ was a smart young man, and he eventually came back home. He agreed to the boundaries. He agreed to the terms. And now he's working two jobs and going to school to be a firefighter.

Later, I was talking to RJ, and he told me the reason he came back home. He said, "I think I knew what I was doing was bad, but I didn't know how bad it was until my own mama said she'd rather not have me home than see me do what I was doing. That hit me hard. That was a wake-up call because I know she loves me unconditionally."

PARENT TRAP #3: THE CONTROL TRAP

Need to know every plan and control every detail so that things will work out your way.

THE FALSE NARRATIVE: "If I don't stay vigilant, something bad will happen."

THE MODUS OPERANDI: Overbearing and overprotective.

THE UNINTENDED MESSAGE TO TEENS: "You can't handle life on your own."

THE ANTIDOTE: Prepare them with the skills required to become responsible without you.

THE HUBRIS CASE STUDY

I immediately noticed how intelligent Carol was, her mind crisp and alert. She was nineteen and had recently graduated from high school, where she got great grades and took multiple AP courses. She was now enrolled in college. The second thing I noticed is that when I asked her a simple question, she always turned to her mother, Jennifer. Jennifer had come to me because her daughter was having trouble adjusting to post-high-school life at the exclusive and prestigious university that she now attended. Jennifer was worried.

"Why don't you like the dorm?" I asked Carol.

"I don't really know," Carol said softly.

"It's just too overwhelming for her," Mom said.

"Ah. What in particular is overwhelming?" I asked Carol.

Carol looked at her mother, as if looking for the right answer.

"There are many things," Mom said.

"Name one," I said, again to Carol. "Just so I can get an idea."

"Well, there's the laundry situation," Mom interjected.

"The laundry situation?" I asked. "*Carol*, perhaps you could tell me about that," I said, trying to drop a hint that Mom should let her daughter answer a question.

"It's just so chaotic," Mom said, not getting the hint.

"Carol, have you ever been taught how to do laundry?" I asked.

Carol looked to her mother.

Mom shook her head. "She was too busy getting good grades in school," she said, laughing nervously.

After a while, I realized that if I wanted to actually talk to Carol, she couldn't be in the same room as her mother. After finally getting her to talk when her mother wasn't around, I realized that now that she was in college, Carol was completely paralyzed by decision-making.

"Indecisive" doesn't even begin to describe it. Carol couldn't make even the simplest, smallest decisions herself.

And do you know why? Because she had never had to. Her mother had always done that for her.

Now, I don't blame Jennifer. She was an immigrant from Vietnam whose family had fled the instability and violence in the region when she was a little girl. And listening to her talk about how her family had lost all its possessions, and how hard they had to work to forge a new life, even in the fertile valley of opportunity in the Bay Area, I empathized with Jennifer's fears.

Jennifer was trying to control every aspect of her family's life so that nothing bad would happen. And eighteen years of doing that (and doing it very well, I might add) resulted in deep and unintended consequences. Carol, her daughter, was unable to problem-solve or process even basic emotions of failure.

The bubble of protection had become the only habitat Carol understood. And when the real world hit—and it always hits—Carol was unprepared.

THE HUMILITY CASE STUDY

Like many adult children of alcoholics, Erick had learned to fight for control in areas of his life where he could while growing up. This was his coping mechanism.

And so when he had kids, it only made sense that Erick was going to fight like mad to ensure that nothing would hurt or harm his kids. That was his self-assigned duty.

When his twelve-year-old daughter was diagnosed with a rare form of cancer, Erick lost his bearings. Although his daughter made a complete recovery, the lingering effect of that diagnosis shook Erick to the core. He went to counseling to attempt to process what was going on, and that's when he had a breakthrough.

"There was a moment with my counselor when he asked me to talk about a time when my father comforted me," Erick told me. "I started talking about how my dad would drive me around to all my basketball practices and to my friend's house, and my counselor stopped me and said, 'I didn't ask you when your dad provided for your needs. I asked you when he comforted you.' And I realized that this had never happened. Not once. And then I realized that I had fallen into the exact same trap. I was so busy protecting and solving my kids' problems that I had never comforted them or helped them process their loss or failure or pain."

Erick eventually realized that his internal dysfunction, though coming from a place of deep concern and deep pain, was actually counterproductive.

He said what helped him was the image from a short story he read while helping his daughter with her SAT prep.

"It was a story about a child who carefully tended to a large jar that contained a caterpillar," Erick told me. "The caterpillar eventually went into a chrysalis. Each day the boy would watch the jar, but as the butterfly emerged, he didn't remove the cocoon from the jar, so that when the butterfly attempted to spread out its wings, it couldn't. The resin then hardened on the butterfly's deformed wings, making it impossible for the creature to fly."

Erick's journey to humility meant realizing that there are a lot of things in life that neither he nor anyone else can control. It meant recognizing that it's unrealistic to think that you can protect other people from pain or suffering or failure. But Erick realized that he could prepare his kids to deal with those things, and that he could be a comforting presence through those tough times when they came. And they always come.

Somehow that would be enough.

PARENT TRAP #4: THE PERFORMANCE TRAP

Need to be recognized as the best. Need to win.

THE FALSE NARRATIVE: "If I don't win, then I'm not worth anything."

THE MODUS OPERANDI: Pressure to perform.

THE UNINTENDED MESSAGE TO TEENS: "You'll never be good enough."

THE ANTIDOTE: Offer encouragement and praise free from achievements. Celebrate your teens for who they are, not what they do.

THE HUBRIS CASE STUDY

Be'anka worked as a counselor and coach at a local high school with a high performance index. The property values of this particular neighborhood were incredibly high, which attracted wealthy and successful families—which in turn meant academic performance was emphasized above nearly all else.

That day Be'anka sat in front of a junior, Emily, and her mom. After looking at the transcripts and talking with Emily and her teachers, Be'anka had a gut feeling that maybe the rigor of all of Emily's college placement classes was taking its toll. Emily thrived in the science classes, but AP literature and history were really dragging her performance down.

Be'anka began her calculated plan to encourage a slightly different academic track for Emily, and gently suggested that she would be better served by concentrating on STEM (science, technology, engineering, and math) courses, and stepping down to regular English or history. But before she could get another syllable out, Emily's mom practically sprang from her seat. The words poured from her as she lit into her daughter.

"You want to drop out?! Move down? Do you honestly think the top-tier colleges will accept you if you take regular senior English? Do you have any idea what that will mean? For your future? If you're not careful, you'll end up . . . well, you'll end up like her," she said, pointing directly at Be'anka. "Is that what you want?"

Recently, I had a chance to sit and listen to a group of parents, school administrators, city officials, and expert psychologists from around the country who met in one of the wealthiest and highest performing school systems in the United States. These adults all had one question before them: What can we do to stop teenagers from this community from throwing themselves in front of oncoming commuter trains? And these adults were not overreacting. Twice in the last five years there had been a suicide cluster of at least five teenagers who had all stepped in front of the same commuter train within the span of a few months.

Suicide clusters—a rare sociological phenomenon defined as a group of three or more suicides in close time or geographic proximity—are exceedingly rare, but they were happening.

A study done at Yale University by Dr. Suniya Luthar found that under extreme academic pressure, teens begin to tie their self-worth to their achievements and see themselves as catastrophically flawed if they don't meet the highest standards of success.

This doesn't mean that every high-pressure academic setting is going to cause teens to commit suicide. But what it does reveal is that these pressure-cooker, performance-driven environments cause teenagers a great deal of suffering.

Back to my friend Be'anka. She excused Emily from the room to attempt to explain to her mom how the messages she was sending to her daughter were destructive. The mother huffed, offended someone would even suggest she would do anything to hurt her daughter.

"What's going to happen to her if she doesn't get into a top-tier school?" Mom asked.

"That's the wrong question," Be'anka shot back. "The better question is 'What will happen to her if she does?'"

THE HUMILITY CASE STUDY

For Lorraine, the move toward humility happened when her daughter, Jenna, quit competitive gymnastics her sophomore year of high school. Now Jenna was not simply good at gymnastics. She was an elite athlete, on track for the world championships and potentially the Olympics.

"I remember I was really angry," Lorraine told me when we sat first down to talk. "I short-circuited. It was completely out of character." Lorraine was surprised at her own anger. I reminded her that anger is nearly always a secondary emotion. What was behind her anger? That was the important question.

"I was never angry, never a taskmaster," Lorraine said. "I wasn't a typical 'helicopter parent,' hovering and yelling at my kids or scolding them. I was positive."

But what Lorraine didn't realize was that even this behavior was setting a culture with her teens. The unspoken message was that if you succeed, you'll get Mom's love and approval and warmth. And if you don't . . . you're out of luck.

For Lorraine, a critical moment came when she sought counsel from Liz, an older mom whom she respected. Liz helped Lorraine unpack some of the emotional issues about her own family, and that's when Lorraine realized that Jenna's gymnastic achievements weren't about her daughter. They were about her and the challenges she herself faced.

"I realized I wanted my kids to win so that I could feel like I was a winner," Lorraine said. "I came from a very high-honor, high-shame family, and the achievement of my kids was all I had to feel good about myself. So if my kids failed, I was a failure as a mom and as a person."

Lorraine's mentor, Liz, also pointed out that her daughter's quitting gymnastics was an incredible act of courage. Most teens feel trapped and have a complete loss of agency in situations of extreme pressure. But Jenna was resolute.

Lorraine remembers the moment when everything clicked for her.

"We were standing in the kitchen, and we were going back and forth, and my daughter said, 'Mom, what's more important? I'm in the gym sixteen hours a week. For the chance to maybe, maybe go to the Olympics? I don't even want to go to the Olympics.' I listened to the things she wanted to do. 'Mom, I want to go to youth group at church and hang out with my friends. I want to be home for dinner with my family.' That really got to me, hearing her beg me to eat dinner with us."

Lorraine humbled herself, worked through her own challenges, and realized that requiring performance without providing emotional support to her daughter wasn't going to work. She figured out that she had to let Jenna be a kid. And so she did.

*   *   *

These four traps are things I've seen over and over again. They hamstring good parents and wind up hurting teens.

The relevant trap for me is number 3, the control trap. I see my own control issues flare up all the time. It's probably because I had so little control over so many things when I was growing up that I seize control now. And that's good sometimes, but other times it's just ugly. Perhaps you can relate.

As a parent, will I ever not have these issues? Honestly, probably not. If I still have them at my age, after all these decades, they're probably not going to fully go away.

But I do need to be aware of my issues. And even if I can't permanently rid myself of these dysfunctions, I need to know what the signs are. I need to know how to put out those fires when they flare up. I need to examine my thoughts, reject bad thinking, and snap out of past behavior. I need to get better.

I know it's tough to stare at your own dysfunctions. But if it's any consolation, being honest with yourself about these things doesn't make you weak. Self-reflection is a door to humility, and if you have the courage to do it, it will make you much stronger and significantly more effective as a parent.

A friend of mine once told me, "The best way to save someone who is drowning in a river is not to jump in the river. It's to remain on solid ground and then to throw that person a sturdy rope."

Let's do our best to remain on solid ground.

A Realistic Path to Humility

I'm fully aware that there's no easy formula for how to become a better person and minimize your character defects. But I wanted to share three steps that I took that helped me (steps that continue to help me). As always, the mileage you get out of these steps may vary, but they are a good starting point for developing humility over hubris.

1. **Consider counseling. Seriously, it's not what you think.**

There are times when that scared, hurt little kid from Oklahoma comes out. And when he does, I know what to do. I go talk to Harrison. He's a trained and licensed counselor, but more important, he's *my* trained and licensed counselor. And he's helped me tremendously because he's given me words to understand my unique dysfunction. He helps me to stop freaking out, get clarity, and become hyperaware of situations that trigger my own weaknesses so that I do not repeat the same unhelpful cycles.

But I also know that sometimes people are hesitant when it comes to counseling. Let me offer two bits of advice.

First, get rid of the narrative that "going to counseling means I'm screwed up." Let's just get this on the table: Everyone is screwed up. *Everyone.* You can try to hide that you're screwed up (thereby isolating yourself, because you can't let people get too close), you can pretend you're not screwed up (upholding an exhausting ruse), or you can compensate (pointing out other people's weaknesses in hopes that no one sees yours). I've done all three. They don't work.

Second, commit in advance to a minimum number of sessions. In the beginning, there's a good chance you'll leave counseling feeling worse than when you arrived. It's like working out in that respect. The soreness is a sign that you're building muscle—that you're making progress.

2. Prioritize intentional friendships.

When I got engaged to my wife, Sarah, one of the things that immediately became apparent to me is that she had *way* more friends than I did. Now, this is partly because she is one of the most extroverted people in the history of humanity.* She encouraged me to make some friends, which was stupid, because I was busy building a career and traveling. I didn't have time for friends. But I humored her.

And that's when I realized. Whoa. I *really* didn't have many friends.

I mean, I had acquaintances. I had people I worked with. I had people I sort of knew from college. I had people who were around. But not really any close friends. And in asking around, I realized that many of us don't, do we?

So, at my wife's urging, I started hanging out with a group of other guys my age, whom I had met while volunteering at our church. That was in 2002. We've now been meeting up nearly every Tuesday night for the past fifteen years.

Like many addicts, I'd withheld the details of my addiction from as many people as I could, creating a false reality. After my epiphany with Jason, these guys were some of the first people I told about my problem with online poker. Just saying it out loud to a group who I knew would not condemn me, but who would do everything in their power to help me, made the painful process far easier. It buoys your heart to know you have that kind of support. It would take another whole book to explain how beneficial this group of guys has been in my life. But I learned that being around good men helped make me a better man. Being around good fathers helped me be a better father. And being around good families helped me have a better family.

---

* This is a woman who knows the life story of our mailman.

3. Form a board of advisers.

There will come a time in your life when you will be faced with a large crisis or issue that you simply cannot figure out on your own. Something in your life will explode. It's not a matter of *if* this will happen. It's a matter of *when*.

And when it happens, you need what I affectionately call a board of advisers. Now, a board of advisers doesn't have to be a big group. It can be as simple as a person or two whom you keep on speed dial. But these people have to have a few things in common:

- They have to be older than you. Probably ten to twenty years older. Experience matters here.
- They have to be people you truly respect. Maybe this goes without saying, but these should be people whom you wouldn't mind being like when you grow up.

Your board of advisers are people you will call when you need specific advice for a specific problem. When there's a big fork in the road and you need wisdom about which way to go. When you need perspective. When you need someone who has done this before and can be your Sherpa to the summit.*

I would not be where I am today if some caring and loving adults had not taken the time to sit down with me and mentor me. And I definitely would not be where I am if I hadn't taken these mentors seriously, listened to their advice, and done everything I could to follow their advice.

---

* Consider this: Personal life coaching is an industry pulling in $1.5 billion a year, and it's growing rapidly. Why? Because there is a lack of mentorship in our country, and people are so desperate for it that they are willing to pay.

Everyone Benefits from a Better You

It's been more than a decade since that online gambling meltdown, and I can honestly say I'm not the same person I was back then. It's taken a lot of work and a few deliberate structures (such as daily text check-ins with accountability partners, software that blocks gambling websites, and removing Internet access on my phone), but because of the help from my wife, my family, my friends, my counselor, Harrison, Tuesday Night Inc., and my mentors, I'm a better person.

A few months ago, as I rifled through the mail on the kitchen counter, I saw there was a postcard for my wife from an organization called MOPS (Mothers of Preschoolers), the motto of which captured my attention. It read: *Better moms make a better world.*

This is true of moms and dads, of all caring adults. And it's really the crux of humility.

Everyone wins when you get better.

> *Humility does not mean you're weak.*
> *It means you're brave.*

Part 2

THE PHASES OF A TEENAGE HUMAN

To help your teen, you have to understand your teen.

With the help of an incredible team of researchers, psychologists, and scientists, and a massive focus group of caring adults, we've distilled the best information about teenagers down to easy-to-read and easy-to-digest snapshots.

These snapshots outline the particular changes that teenagers undergo at every age from eleven to eighteen. We've also outlined exactly what teens need from grown-ups at each stage, and the key actions you can take to provide what they need.

PROPERLY DIAGNOSING YOUR TEEN

Phil hates hospitals. You see, when he was a kid, he spent nine days in a row in a hospital, watching his three-year-old little brother, Timmy, get sicker and sicker and sicker.

Nine days and nine nights.

Timmy went into the hospital complaining of a stomachache. His condition deteriorated. Soon he was awake but couldn't lift his eyelids. Then he started drifting in and out of consciousness. They had to put Timmy on a respirator to help him breathe. The doctors ran dozens of tests, desperately checking for anything they could think of. All the tests came back inconclusive.

Enter Dr. Langmead.

Dr. Langmead was the family physician, and he also happened to do rounds at the hospital. Like all the other doctors, he was baffled by Timmy's condition, but Dr. Langmead took this personally. At one point, he sat down with a large yellow legal pad and interviewed the entire family. He asked them to recall everything they could about the week before Timmy had come into the hospital. Any detail, no matter how insignificant it seemed. Dr. Langmead was a detective, looking for clues.

Phil's dad was emotional recalling the night before Timmy had been admitted. At dinner, they'd had Timmy's favorite food—fish sticks—but Timmy had been difficult that night, refusing to eat his vegetables. So, as a consequence, they had sent him to bed early before he had finished his fish sticks. Later Timmy snuck downstairs to try to eat the fish sticks, but his mom had already thrown them away.

"I remember carrying him up the stairs, and he was crying, 'Daddy, I want more fish sticks,'" Phil's dad recalled, eyes filled with tears. "Why didn't I just let him have the fish sticks?"

And that was all Dr. Langmead needed. He leaped up off the couch and ran down the hall of the hospital.

"I think I know what's wrong with Timmy," Dr. Langmead said as he called for the head nurse and the attending physician. "His favorite food was fish sticks. I bet he snuck downstairs and ate the fish sticks that had been thrown away in the trash. Timmy has botulism. We can treat botulism!"

And Dr. Langmead was right. Within twenty-four hours, Timmy was almost completely better. Treating foodborne botulism is pretty straightforward, but it requires an accurate diagnosis.

In reviewing twenty-five years of US malpractice claims, Johns Hopkins researchers found that diagnostic errors—not surgical mistakes or medication overdoses—accounted for the largest fraction of claims. In fact, misdiagnosis might be the single biggest patient safety issue in the United States. More than one hundred thousand people per year are misdiagnosed, and diagnosis-related malpractice suits amounted to $38.8 billion in the last thirty years.

In my experience in working with teenagers, I've found a similar parallel.

The most effective parents, teachers, and caring adults exhibit the same dogged determination as Dr. Langmead. They do the hard work to understand what's really going on in the heart and head of a teenager so that they correctly diagnose the situation.

Teens are rapidly changing humans. But we have to accurately diagnose what's going on with them so that we can best help them.

Good news: That's what this section of the book is about.

In the following pages, you will find easy-to-digest and easy-to-implement summaries that outline the particular changes teenagers undergo at every age from eleven to eighteen. These were developed in partnership with the Just a Phase Project,[*] a collaborative, ongoing effort combining innovative research with practical application. In addition, we assembled a team of researchers, psychologists, counselors, and youth workers, and a massive focus group of parents, teachers, and caring adults to distill the best information about teenagers at every age. These summaries pull from that information and highlight exactly what teens need most, and how parents can take action to give them what they need at each phase.

The goal is simple. Be like Dr. Langmead. Use the best information available to understand what's going on with teenagers so that we as caring adults can be more effective at helping them.

Because just as was true in the story of Timmy and Dr. Langmead, you never know when paying close attention to the details could make all the difference.

[*] Learn more at ParentThePhase.com.

Naive. Changing. Insecure.

THE "WHO LIKES ME?" PHASE

Teen's Focus: Acceptance

They have entered into a time when things begin changing—their friends, their hobbies, their moods, and even their voice. It's easier for them to navigate all these changes when they know they're not alone.

Grown-Up's Role: Provide Stability

With so much change happening, try to minimize uncertainties. Providing reliable emotional support, transportation, and meals will mean more than you know.

Key Actions

- Make this time count. Kids at this age still *really* want to be with you.
- Plan adventures. Brainstorm meaningful activities together. (Think: a preteen bucket list.)
- Enjoy books, movies, and music together, which can kick-start meaningful conversations about life.
- Talk about adult life. Talk about your biggest adventures and mistakes. They're listening.
- Discuss the birds and the bees. Answer any question they ask in detail. If you don't, Google will.

At This Age . . .

THEY THINK LIKE ENGINEERS.
So connect the dots for them.

THEY ARE MOTIVATED BY ACCEPTANCE.
So affirm their personal journey.

Research Shows They Are Changing . . .

PHYSICALLY

- Need a lot of food and nine to eleven hours of sleep each night.
- Continue to lose molars (ages nine to twelve).
- Girls begin outpacing boys in development.
- Boys experience changes in height and weight, an increase in hormones, and possible acne.
- Girls experience changes in height and body shape and may begin menstruation (ages ten to sixteen).

MENTALLY

- Enjoy learning new skills and being challenged.
- Increasingly able to grasp abstract concepts like justice.
- Growing ability to see the world from different perspectives.
- Struggle to discern another person's motive for their actions.
- Sudden brain growth may lead to forgetfulness.

RELATIONALLY

- Debate often, but argue more from emotion than logic.
- Seek peer approval and conformity.

- Often display worst behavior at home.
- Benefit from having a same-gender best friend.
- Value nonparental adult influences.
- May have romantic interests and experiment with physical affection.

EMOTIONALLY

- Often mask emotions in order to fit in.
- Benefit from talking about feelings.
- Struggle with decision-making.
- Lie more than at any other phase.
- May become preoccupied with perceived abilities and undervalue persistence and practice.

Approximately 364 Weeks Until Graduation . . .

Curious. Excitable. Uncertain.

THE "WHO AM I?" PHASE

Teen's Focus: Identity

They're in a phase of self-discovery. Their interests and abilities may change, and for the first time, not everyone makes the team. They have new questions about who they are and what they believe.

Grown-Up's Role: Highlight Emerging Strengths

Many voices and mediums will try to shape their identity—some positive, some negative. They need someone to affirm their strengths, deny their misconceptions, and help them discover their uniqueness.

Key Actions

- Be encouraging. Make a point to say something encouraging daily.
- Drive them where they need to go. Soon the opportunity for car conversations will end.
- Coauthor a set of rules together. A clear set of written rules with their buy-in establishes you as a fair authority.
- Follow them respectfully. Stay connected digitally and physically— but give them space.
- Name their uniqueness. If you don't help them clarify their identity, someone else will.

At This Age . . .

THEY THINK LIKE ENGINEERS.
So connect the dots for them.

THEY ARE MOTIVATED BY ACCEPTANCE.
So affirm their personal journey.

Research Shows They Are Changing . . .

PHYSICALLY

- Still need nine to eleven hours of sleep each night and may easily fatigue or develop headaches.
- Girls outpace boys in development.
- Guys experience changes in height and body shape and may develop body odor, body hair, and increased muscle mass.
- Girls experience a significant growth spurt and the development of body odor, body hair, and breasts. Menstruation is likely (ages ten to sixteen).

MENTALLY

- Capable of self-evaluation and self-critique.
- Able to see two sides of an argument.
- Connect information to form an opinion.
- Solve multistep, complex problems.
- Growing ability to organize their mind, but maybe not their bedroom.

RELATIONALLY

- Often interested in pop culture, slang, or current events.
- Want to negotiate rules and test boundaries.
- Display an increasingly adultlike personality.
- Need nonparental adult influences.
- Benefit from having a same-gender best friend.

EMOTIONALLY

- Enjoy sarcasm and sophisticated jokes.
- Often interested in leadership roles and teaching younger kids.
- May emphasize physical appearance and performance.
- Tend to overschedule their time.
- Benefit from talking about feelings.

Approximately 312 Weeks Until Graduation . . .

Social. Impulsive. Searching.

THE "WHERE DO I BELONG?" PHASE

Teen's Focus: Friends

This is the age when most teenagers begin high school. As small fish in a bigger pond, they can easily feel overlooked. The drive for peer connection and adult recognition is heightened in this phase.

Grown-Up's Role: Know Their Community

Teens this age gravitate to where they find acceptance, but over the next four years no one will influence their decisions like their friends. So pay close attention to their influences. Help them choose and analyze friends wisely.

Key Actions

- Prioritize healthy friendships. Figure out where positive influences gather and use your influence to get them into that environment.
- Help them be a good friend. Discuss what it means to take initiative, be authentic, offer forgiveness, and develop the other skills that make a good friend. Use examples from your own life.
- Remember that you have veto power. Use it sparingly, but if necessary, remove negative influences *before* they become entrenched.

- Give them hope. Nothing that happens this year changes their worth or has to determine their future.
- Widen the circle. Invite other trusted adults to spend time with them.

At This Age . . .

THEY THINK LIKE PHILOSOPHERS.
So ask questions.

THEY ARE MOTIVATED BY FREEDOM.
So give them choices whenever possible.

Research Shows They Are Changing . . .

PHYSICALLY

- Have difficulty falling asleep before eleven P.M. (it's biological).
- Need nine hours of sleep and one hour of exercise per day.
- Girls still outpace boys in development.
- Guys are getting taller, smellier, and hairier, and gaining muscle mass; may also experience an increase in acne, voice changes, and weird dreams.
- Girls' bodies take on adult physical appearance; after menstruation, increase in height will slow and then stop.

MENTALLY

- Increasingly able to focus, recall, and organize information.
- Overly self-aware; may think "everybody's watching me."
- Wired for risk-taking and sensational experiences.
- Resistant to potentially embarrassing situations.
- "I am bored" often means "I don't understand."

RELATIONALLY

- Girls begin wearing makeup on a regular basis.
- Dating relationships tend to be short-lived.
- Increased interest in sexual expression (30 percent report being sexually active).
- Say they want parents to listen more than advise.

EMOTIONALLY

- Feel empowered through choices rather than rules.
- May still feel insecure about their changing body.
- Need help navigating extreme emotions.
- May experience changes in motivation.
- Seek experiences that create intense feelings and emotions.
- Increasingly vulnerable to addiction: self-harm, alcohol, pornography, etc.

Approximately 208 Weeks Until Graduation . . .

Contrarian. Risk-Taking. Experimental.

THE "WHY CAN'T I?" PHASE

Teen's Focus: Freedom

At this phase, teens begin questioning whether there's more to life than what they've seen and experienced. And the more they begin to experience personally, the more they may question the advice of well-intentioned authorities.

Grown-Up's Role: Clarify Their Values

As their freedom increases, risky and sometimes self-destructive behavior has the potential to escalate. Help teens clarify their values, establish personal boundaries, and navigate failure and consequences.

Key Actions

- Enlist other caring adults. Intentionally surround your teens with adults who will help them gain a healthy perspective.
- Lean in. Even though they push you away, fight for their heart. Write them a card; send them a text; take them out to lunch unexpectedly. Make time to have fun together.
- Maintain consistent consequences. Collaborate on clear rules and expectations and, when possible, predetermined consequences. Guardrails are key.
- Talk about dating. Whether or not they are dating, they have

opinions about it. Give them opportunities to talk about their
dating values with you in a nonthreatening environment.
- Look for adventures. Rather than limiting their experience, look
  for, encourage, and place them in situations where they will be
  challenged and their potential can be expanded.

At This Age . . .

THEY THINK LIKE PHILOSOPHERS.
So ask questions.

THEY ARE MOTIVATED BY FREEDOM.
So give them choices whenever possible.

Research Shows They Are Changing . . .

PHYSICALLY

- Have difficulty falling asleep before eleven P.M. (it's biological).
- Need nine hours of sleep and one hour of exercise per day.
- Girls have likely reached adult height and body development.
- Guys may experience an increase in acne, voice changes, and
  weird dreams.

MENTALLY

- Increasingly able to focus, recall, and organize information.
- Keenly aware of global issues and may be critical of the adult
  world.
- Overly self-aware; may think "everybody's watching me."
- Wired for risk-taking and sensational experiences.
- Tend to be curious, inquisitive, and drawn toward the supernat-
  ural.

RELATIONALLY

- Dating relationships may become more "committed."
- Increased interest in sexual expression (41 percent report being sexually active).
- Increased susceptibility to date violence and rape (age sixteen).
- May experience depression; highest chance of teen suicide in these years.
- Desire respect and responsibilities that increase freedom; may enjoy sharing ideas with adults who will listen.

EMOTIONALLY

- Feel empowered through choices rather than rules.
- Respond well to specific praise.
- Becoming aware of their personal tendencies and patterns.
- Need help navigating extreme emotions.
- Seek experiences that create intense feelings and emotions.
- Vulnerable to addiction: self-harm, alcohol, pornography, etc.

Approximately 156 Weeks Until Graduation . . .

Differentiating. Idealistic. Dreamer.

THE "HOW CAN I MATTER?" PHASE

Teen's Focus: Distinction

At this phase, teens are becoming more keenly aware of their own strengths and weaknesses and how they are different from their peers. They are often interested in greater social causes, and they are eager to make a contribution.

Grown-Up's Role: Refine Their Skills

This is a pressure-filled year when freedom collides with responsibility. Help them discover opportunities to test their interests, stretch their abilities, and better identify their uniqueness.

Key Actions

- Identify what you see as their unique skills and character traits, and call those things out.
- Have others chime in as well. Invite other trusted adults to identify what unique skills and character traits they see.
- "You're not acting like you." Discourage negative behavior by pointing out that it's a violation of their own values.
- Don't discourage dreaming. Even if it seems unrealistic. They are test-driving ideas.

- Your job has changed. Understand your role has shifted from air traffic controller to coach.

At This Age . . .

THEY THINK LIKE PHILOSOPHERS.
So ask questions.

THEY ARE MOTIVATED BY FREEDOM.
So give them choices whenever possible.

Research Shows They Are Changing . . .

PHYSICALLY

- Have difficulty falling asleep before eleven P.M. (it's biological).
- Need nine hours of sleep and one hour of exercise per day.
- Girls have likely reached adult height and body development.
- Guys may continue to grow in height, and develop muscle mass and body and facial hair.

MENTALLY

- Can be insightful and incisive about complex issues.
- Wired for risk-taking and sensational experiences.
- Tend to be opportunistic and idealistic.
- Struggle with long-term thinking.
- Expanding mental capabilities to grasp paradox, hyperbole, innuendo, and satire.

RELATIONALLY

- Dating relationships may become more "committed."
- Increased interest in sexual expression (54 percent report being sexually active).
- Care about issues like control, responsibility, and freedom (both personally and globally).
- Tend to be self-focused, busy, and unavailable.

EMOTIONALLY

- Value humor as a positive point of connection.
- Becoming more at ease with who they are; may become more honest than in previous phases.
- Often take on more than they can handle.
- May struggle with regulating their emotions.

Approximately 104 Weeks Until Graduation . . .

Future-Focused. Autonomous. Afraid.

THE "WHAT WILL I DO?" PHASE

Teen's Focus: Graduation

They are outgrowing high school and are likely to show it through a lack of interest in school-related activities. Instead, the inevitability of life after high school becomes their primary focus. They are simultaneously ready for the future to begin and anxious about what it holds.

Grown-Up's Role: Focus Their Options

Nothing is as overwhelming as "you can be anything" or as disheartening as "you have no options." Most teens this age fall somewhere in between, so help them prepare for the future by identifying positive, realistic options.

Key Actions

- Calm them down. Communicate that they don't have to figure out their entire life right now.
- Focus on baby steps. Help them identify the first few steps they can take.
- Discuss career interests. Help them investigate and test-drive those interests.
- Don't bail them out. Prepare them for the future by letting them clean up their own mistakes.

- They are about to inherit unparalleled amounts of freedom, so wherever appropriate hand over that freedom and give them ownership. Continue to advise them in areas where they struggle most.

At This Age . . .

THEY THINK LIKE PHILOSOPHERS.
So ask questions.

THEY ARE MOTIVATED BY FREEDOM.
So give them choices whenever possible.

Research Shows They Are Changing . . .

PHYSICALLY

- Wisdom teeth may begin to come in (age seventeen to twenty-one).
- Have difficulty falling asleep before eleven P.M. (it's biological).
- Need nine hours of sleep and one hour of exercise per day.
- Girls have likely reached adult height and body development.
- Guys may continue to grow in height, and develop muscle mass and body and facial hair.

MENTALLY

- May overly romanticize or catastrophize.
- Open to discussing current affairs and social issues.
- Capable of solving complex, multistep problems.

RELATIONALLY

- Increased interest in sexual expression (64 percent report being sexually active).
- Less available for family time.
- Want to feel ownership over personal decisions.
- Show respect for others' opinions and are able to compromise.
- More at ease around adults.

EMOTIONALLY

- Becoming more emotionally stable, but still need support and grace.
- Often thrive in a particular area of interest.
- Value being true to themselves.
- Frequently demonstrate initiative for personal interests.

Approximately 52 Weeks Until Graduation . . .

Part 3

TROUBLESHOOTING COMMON TEENAGE CHALLENGES

The following section is unflinchingly practical and designed to help you with common challenges you'll likely face with your very own teenage human.

Think of this section like a cookbook, where you can flip to exactly what you're dealing with and find step-by-step directions. Only instead of trying to figure out how to make an award-winning blueberry crumble, you're trying to figure out what to do if your teen flunks four classes or comes home drunk.

Good times.

FADE IN: *EXT. HOUSE—LATE AFTERNOON*
A nondescript suburban house.
DISSOLVE TO: *INT., HOUSE KITCHEN*
MIGUEL, a sixteen-year-old, is sitting at the island in the kitchen.
He's doing some sort of homework. He is listening to music through
earbuds. He absentmindedly wiggles a pencil and shoves pretzel
sticks into his mouth while he studies.
DISSOLVE TO: *INT., HALLWAY LEADING INTO KITCHEN*
ANGIE, a Latina mom, walks into the kitchen. She is smiling and
pleasant.

ANGIE: Hey, hon.
MIGUEL: (*Taking earbuds out, a bit confused*) Hey, Mom.
ANGIE: So it's that time.
MIGUEL: Time for what? Did I forget . . . ?
ANGIE: I just got an email reminder from my nagging club.
MIGUEL: Nagging club?
ANGIE: Yeah. It's called Nagaste. Anyway, it's time for me to
nag you.
MIGUEL: Oh, you don't have to . . .
ANGIE: Yes, so here goes. (*Pulling out a list and reading without*
emotion, a bit like she is reading a phone book, as if she just has to get

through the list) For the fiftieth time, would you please take out the trash? Why are you playing video games? Have you done all your homework? For the love of God, clean your room—it smells like a locker room in there. Don't raise your voice at me. Do you want to see my C-section scars? Because you hurt me less then than your words do right now.

MIGUEL: Wow.

ANGIE: Well, if I don't remind you about the most important things in life, I'm afraid that you'll forget them.

MIGUEL: I don't think that's true.

ANGIE: No, it is. If I don't nag you, you'll wind up pregnant under a bridge.

MIGUEL: Unlikely.

ANGIE: (*Quickly, with passion*) Statistically that is what they say will happen.

MIGUEL: Wait, who is "they"?

ANGIE: I have to influence your choices, and this is the only way to accomplish it.

MIGUEL: I don't think that's how it works.

ANGIE: You're right. I also have to get really emotional and yell so that you understand that I'm serious.

MIGUEL: Uh-oh.

ANGIE: (*Yelling pretty loudly the same list, with emotion*) For the love of God, clean your room—it smells like a locker room in there!

MIGUEL: (*Cutting her off*) Mom, Mom, Mom, this isn't working. I just want to tune you out.

ANGIE: No. No, you can't tune me out because of the sheer volume of my nagging.

MIGUEL: Do you mean volume like amount, or volume like decibel level?

ANGIE: Yes.

MIGUEL: Again, I don't think that's how it works.

ANGIE: Well, you've never been married to your father.

MIGUEL: Mom, what if we just talked about what we both want, and made promises t—

ANGIE: No. Only nagging. It's what my mom did, so I'm going to do it, too.

MIGUEL: Okay. So when you nag, do you mind if I roll my eyes and tune you out?

ANGIE: Sure. Now brush your teeth, and make sure you don't get pregnant.

MIGUEL: Uh.

INT., HOUSE HALLWAY

NARRATOR: Tired of nagging? Not seeing the results with your teen that you hoped? Well, this section will show you how to stop losing your cool when your teenager doesn't listen, and how to stop lecturing and nagging. It will also give you some easy-to-understand and easy-to-implement tools that will dramatically improve respect, closeness, and influence with your teenager. Keep reading. Don't be like Angie.

Getting Them to Take Ownership and Apologize

The Challenge

"To err is human," wrote the great English poet Alexander Pope. But many people forget the second half of that famous line, which is "to forgive, divine." Learning how to ask for forgiveness is not just important for healthy relationships, it is crucial. When your teens mess up—and they will mess up (I mean, didn't you as a teen?)—they could use the help of a caring adult. Whether they offended a friend, disrespected an authority figure, or stole from your purse, here's what you can do to turn the situation from one marked with shame, insecurity, and embarrassment into an exercise that can more fully develop empathy and maturity.

Your Goal

Raise a teenager who can take ownership for his or her actions and apologize in a way that's both emotionally authentic and improves the chance of reconciliation.

What to Expect

"I DIDN'T DO ANYTHING WRONG."

Your teenager might be stubborn and refuse to admit he or she is wrong.* More often than not, this is because they're scared and insecure. They already have fragile self-esteem, and apologizing can feel like admitting inadequacy—which makes them feel even more vulnerable to rejection.

Here are two things you could say that might help:

- "I don't know. You might need to do a gut check here. It sounds to me like what you did actually hurt someone you care about. Do you think I'm wrong about that?"
- "I have found in my life that it takes far more courage and strength for me to apologize than it does not to apologize. Do you agree with that?"

"WELL, I NEVER WOULD HAVE _____ IF THEY HADN'T _____."

There will likely be a situation where both parties did something wrong. Frustratingly, your teen will focus entirely on how he or she was wronged and will go to extraordinary lengths to justify his or her own actions. You have to defuse this bomb carefully, and one of the ways to do this is to differentiate between a reason and an excuse. A reason is a factor that helps explain why your teen acted the way he or

---

* This is not just a teenage thing. I once had a friend who apologized by saying, "This is not the most right I've ever been." Then he got married, and now he's *great* at apologizing.

she did. This is useful to examine, but help your teen see that a reason is never an excuse or a justification, and that nobody ever *makes* you react a certain way.* No one has that power, because all of us are solely responsible for our own actions, words, thoughts, and emotions.

Here are some questions to get to the heart of that distinction:

- "Tell me your side of the story. What happened?"
- "What were you feeling in the situation? What factors do you think triggered your reaction?"
- "Okay, I think I've heard some of the reasons that led you to do what you did. And those might be good reasons to be upset, but do you think those reasons are an excuse for your actions?"

"I LITERALLY DON'T KNOW WHAT I DID WRONG."

It's possible that your teenager will legitimately not understand what he or she did wrong. Teenagers notoriously misinterpret social situations and communication, and it's possible that the whole situation is a giant misunderstanding.

Here are two helpful sentences you can arm teens with if they're stuck, to help them talk to the person with whom they're having a conflict:

- "I feel like there's tension between us, and I've been thinking about it for a long time. I wonder if I did something to upset you? Is there something I should apologize for?"
- "I'm sorry that we're fighting. I really am. I truly value you as a friend. And if there's something I did to upset you, I'd like to hear it so I can apologize to you."

---

* Except for the dulcet tones of Michael Bublé. No man, woman, or child alive can resist the wave of emotions induced by that modern-day crooner.

What to Do

1. **Encourage empathy.** Coach your teen to really, truly focus on the other person. An apology is a "regretful acknowledgment of an offense or failure." The point of apologizing is to acknowledge that you have done something that has caused harm to someone else and damaged the relationship. In order to effectively apologize, teens must refocus their thoughts toward others.

Ask your teen the following questions:

- What happened?
- Why do you think the other person is upset?
- Do you think they have a right to be upset?
- How would you feel if it were you?

2. **Push for evaluation.** Coach teens to evaluate their own actions. One thing that most teens are great at is evaluating the morality of what other people have done to them. What they are *not* good at is evaluating what they have done. Your job is to slow down and ask some questions that will allow them to evaluate their actions. Ideally, they'll come to the conclusion that what they did was wrong.

Ask your teen these questions to help lead to self-reflection:

- Now that the emotion of the moment is over, when you look back at it, do you wish you had said or done things differently?
- Do you think what you did was right, or could you have done something better?
- How would you react if someone treated you the way you treated that person?

3. **Promote maturity (and making the first move).** Coach your teen to act with maturity. Many teenagers feel that by making the move to

apologize, they are admitting that the whole situation is their fault. Your role is to show them that this is not true. Even in a situation where your teen is only 5 percent wrong and the other person is 95 percent wrong, show him or her that maturity means taking 100 percent responsibility for that 5 percent. And then encourage your teen to make the first move by initiating the apology.

Help your teen see that part of the reason we apologize is to show that we highly value the other person and our relationship with him or her. Explain that it takes more courage and maturity to make the first move.

4. **Help make amends.** It's possible that what your teen did has consequences. You have to help your teen to be ready to do whatever it takes to make things right. Help him or her brainstorm about whether there are reparations needed.

Remind your teen that it may:

- Cost money: If your teen borrowed his or her friend's phone and dropped the phone in the river, he or she will have to save up and buy the friend a new phone.
- Cost time: If they forgot to do something they promised they would do, they will have to stop what they're doing now and honor that commitment.
- Cost ego: If your teen said something untrue about someone, he or she might have to get up and apologize to the group or class.

5. **Support letting things go.** One of the most difficult things for teens to do is to drop their expectations about how someone else is going to receive the apology. After each apology, we truly hope the other person sees our sincerity, sees our plans to change, and says, "I accept your apology and I forgive you." But it might not go that way. The other person might not accept your apology and might need time. He or she might say, "No way! I don't forgive you! I'll never forgive you for what you've done."

It often takes more maturity to accept an apology than deliver one. Ask teens the following questions to help them process what to do in case their apology is not accepted:

- After you deliver this apology, how do you hope the other person will respond? What would be the best-case scenario?
- Do you think it's possible the other person might not react the way you hope? What would that look like?
- What will you do if the other person responds in a way that isn't what you and I are hoping for? What kinds of things could you say?

Remind your teen that apologizing is his or her responsibility, but the response to the apology is the other person's job. Teenagers need to understand they can control only one side. They've done what they needed to do, with courage, honesty, and humility. If the other person refuses to accept the apology and continues on in anger and bitterness, that's not your teen's fault. That's on the other person. Sometimes the only response is something simple like this:

I'm very sorry you feel that way. I hope you can forgive me someday. I really do value you.

The Breakdown of an Effective Apology

Writing out apologies has a few key benefits. It ensures that you don't stammer or forget something important because you're nervous. It allows you to do the hard work of thinking about what you've done, and it forces you to be precise with the words you use to apologize.

Here's a step-by-step guide to the components of a sincere and effective apology.

PART 1: Start off by stating your clear intent to apologize. This disarms the other person and creates a less tense environment.

Dear Olivia,

I wanted to apologize to you. I wrote this apology down to make sure I said things correctly.

PART 2: Be as specific as you can in describing the moment of the offense.

When I asked you if you wanted to go to the Snack Shack while you were with your friends at the varsity basketball game the other day, I didn't realize that if I offered to buy you something, your friends would think that I was asking you out on a date, or your friends would think that I "liked" you.

I also need to apologize because after you reacted the way you did, I didn't know what to do. I knew that I needed to apologize to you, but I didn't have the courage or the right words. I should have just left and given you your space, instead of hanging around near you and your friends. I was trying to do the right thing by apologizing to you, but I realize now that I made things worse.

PART 3: Let the other person know that you tried to take his or her perspective. Show that you understand the effect your actions or words had on someone else (even if it was an accident).

Thinking about it from your perspective, I can imagine that you were embarrassed in front of your friends. Although I never meant for that to happen, and I didn't know your friends would interpret things that way, I can see now that what I did put you in an awkward situation.

PART 4: Use the word "that" instead of "if." For example, "I am sorry that I hurt your feelings" is better than "I am sorry if I hurt your feelings." There's no "if" about it. It happened. By using the word "that," you show that you're taking responsibility.

I am sorry that what I did embarrassed you and made you feel awkward.

PART 5: This is the most important part of the apology. Outline a clear plan for changing. This shows you take the situation seriously. The last thing you want to be is the kind of person who apologizes for the same thing over and over again.

> *In order to make sure this doesn't happen again:*
> *I'll respect your privacy and I won't approach you by myself when you're with your friends.*
> *I won't invite you to do something unless your brother is also joining me.*
> *In those cases, I'll have your brother be the one to ask you if you want to join us and come along.*

PART 6: Ask for their patience. When you tell someone you are going to try to change, be sure and say something to the effect of "But I might mess up every now and then, so please be patient with me because I really do want to work on this." Most people will be very patient because they know you're trying. They don't expect perfection—they just want progress.

> *And if I do something that embarrasses you, please be patient with me and let me know, because I really want to be a good friend to you.*

PART 7: Affirm the importance of the other person and your relationship.

> *Thanks for listening to me, and I really do hope you can forgive me. You're my best friend's sister, after all, and I think you're an awesome person.*

HOW TO CRAFT AN EFFECTIVE APOLOGY

Now that we have broken down all the essential components of an apology, it's time for your teen to craft his or her own following this easy-to-use template.

1. Briefly write out what you did or said that was wrong and hurtful.

   PROMPT: What exactly happened, and what did I do that was wrong?

2. Disclose what you did that hurt the other person. Put yourself in the other person's shoes. Make a list of how your actions might have made the other person feel. How would you have felt if the tables were turned?

   PROMPT: How did what I do hurt the other person?

3. Explain what you plan on doing and changing. If you love someone and have done something to hurt him or her, then love means stopping that thing. Immediately (as best you can). Figure out what the next step is, and then tell the person you're apologizing to.

   PROMPT: What do I need to do to make things right?

What to Do When They Blow Your Trust

The Challenge

If you're like most parents, you have rules. And it's likely you spend a lot of time talking about those rules with your teenager, because you hope those rules will help your teen become a certain type of person. Now, if your teen breaks those rules out of ignorance or due to an accident or carelessness, that's one thing. It's quite another for your teen to do something in willful and knowing defiance of the rules you spent dozens of hours reviewing ad nauseam. This drives us parents nuts.* And it really does put a strain on the relationship. But if failure is inevitable for everyone, then letting kids fail early and often—and giving them the chance to learn from their failures in safe and supportive environments—is the best way to help them grow. Here's how to make that happen.

Your Goal

Use your teen's foolish mistake as a way to improve honest communication and guide your teen toward healthy self-governance. Then provide a clear plan to rebuild trust.

---

* It's at times like this that I harken back to the words of my tenderhearted, angelic grandmother, who said—and I quote—"It's not wrong to want to tase that child. It's the doing such that's a felony." Sage words, Nana. Sage words.

What to Expect

At some point, your teen will blow your trust. This will happen to you.

Teenagers, by definition, are not adults. They make mistakes. They don't think things through. They make bad decisions. Think about when you were a teenager: Did you ever do something half-thought-out or just plain idiotic or wrong, something that is rather cringe-worthy looking back at it? Of course you did. So expect that this is coming.

When your teen messes up, you should also expect that he or she is going to compound this error with another and lie to you. And teens usually lie for one of these two reasons:

Self-preservation. They are afraid of getting in trouble, so they hide the evidence, omit key details, or straight-up tell you things that are untrue. This isn't because they are pathological socio-paths intent on destroying civilization. It's because they are scared.

Because they value you. Teens know instinctively when they do something that will disappoint you, so they lie to attempt to hide it from you because there is nothing worse than looking into the eyes of someone we love and seeing disappointment. Try to look beneath the actions to their motives.

Your teen might pretend otherwise, but your opinion of them carries tremendous weight.* And whether they show it or not, they are probably scared. They aren't stupid; they know they blew it. They are

---

* If you doubt this, please refer to Mindset #1: Teens Need You More Than It Seems.

looking for clues on how to restore your trust and restore the relationship, and they need a clear plan. It's true that knowing when to trust
someone again is pretty subjective. But the steps that people need to
take tend to be concrete and straightforward. So give your teen clear
next steps.

What to Do

1. **Change your perspective: What if this is a good thing?** We get it.
Your teen has messed up, and you're upset. Maybe what they've done
is just stupid, or maybe they've gone and done something that violates
every single value you've tried to teach them for the last decade and
a half, and you can feel yourself turning into the Hulk just thinking
about the situation.

But what if this isn't about you at all? What if this is a golden opportunity to get a glimpse into what's going on beneath the surface of
your teen's life? What if you leverage this debacle in a way that could
lead to some honest conversation? Was your teen caught drinking at
a party? Maybe he's struggling to find and listen to the right friends
(and maybe he knows it). Did they blow up at you over something triv-
ial? There's likely something going on that they're not talking about.
Did they post a photo of themselves in their underwear? Maybe they
feel insecure and are trying to get (the wrong kind of!) attention.

2. **Do the difficult work of defusing your own anger, disappointment,
and fear.** When your teen does something immature, dangerous, or
stupid, it can trigger your anger. But anger is usually the tip of the
emotional iceberg, with hurt, disappointment, rejection, fear, or humiliation underneath. What are you feeling? Why are you feeling it?

The goal here is to compose yourself, which, depending on the situation, might mean you need to remove yourself from the presence
of your teen for a few minutes. A good line to use might be "I heard
what you said, and I appreciate your words. But I need a few minutes
to think about all this."

Questions to consider:

- If I am honest, this episode upset me because_____.
- I am afraid that this incident means _____.
- I am most concerned about _____.

3. **Your teen expects the hammer. Surprise him or her with vulnerability.** Your teen thinks the thing you want most is to punish her by grounding her until she's thirty. And there's likely a side of you that wants to do that—even if that means she'd still be living with you through her twenties.

There will likely be very real consequences. But what if all of that is secondary? Your teen knows that a conversation is going to happen. But what if you used all your leverage to talk honestly about the event, and the fears and concerns you have? What if you openly shared the "why" driving your anger, so that your teenager could see behind the scenes and realize that you aren't mad because she broke "your rules" but because you are genuinely worried about her well-being?

Use the sentences below as conversation prompts to get the ball rolling:

- I'm worried that _____ might happen if _____.
- I'm concerned about _____.
- What scares me most is _____.

Remember: Vulnerability leads to vulnerability.

4. **Ask your teen: "What do you think should happen next? How can we* make this right?"** Involving the teen in the discussion about consequences is a sound approach. And a vast majority of adults say that

---

* First off, notice the "we" language. That's done on purpose. Using the word "you" is technically more accurate, but it puts your teen on the defensive.

what their teen came up with as a punishment was much more severe than what they had been thinking.

Make sure the consequence the teen comes up with is a natural consequence, not a non sequitur. The point is to establish a clear link between actions, the erosion of trust, and consequences, not simply self-flagellation.

> **Non sequitur:** I took your car without permission, so for the month of May, I will have to clean all the bathrooms in the house with my toothbrush.

> **Natural consequence:** If your teen takes your car without permission, a better punishment is that he or she can't drive anywhere without you for a month or two, or doesn't get to borrow the car for a certain period of time.

5. **Teach them to accelerate trust by overcommunicating.** Teach teens that if they want to rebuild trust, they need to overcommunicate with you. Ask them to inquire about their chores, then communicate with you when they have completed assigned tasks. Ask them to let you know where they are going to be, when they arrive at a destination, what they're doing, what they are planning to do next, and when they will be home. Explain to your teen that this overcommunication tells the adults in your life, "I want you to trust me again."

6. **Ask the question "What did we learn from this?"** One of your primary roles is to develop your relationship with your teen in order to help him or her toward a healthy and productive self-governance. A key way to do this is to guide him or her through some self-reflection.

Try asking your teen:

- What was most difficult for you during this whole thing?
- How will I know when you are acting more trustworthy and honest?
- What did you learn about yourself from this episode?
- If you had to go back and do this all again, what would you change?
- What do you want me to know that you don't think I know?

Setting Up Clearly Written House Rules

The Challenge

Your teen broke curfew. Again. It's 11:48 P.M. at the end of a very difficult day—and you are fuming. "Who has time for this?" you ask yourself.

"Not me," you respond to yourself, because you are a pleasure to talk to.

"Plus, I am worried sick," you say (to you).

"What if they are in a ditch somewhere?" you add, starting to sound a bit like your mother.

You are now a Mount Vesuvius of rage, and when that kid walks through that door, you are going to blow. You will take away the car keys, cancel the cell phone plan, ground him or her for six months, even change the Wi-Fi password while you're at it.

At 11:52 P.M., your teen shuffles in. You (understandably) yell and threaten. Your teenage human mutters a defensive excuse and heads directly to his or her room. Deflated and exhausted, you go to bed as well. And when you wake up in the morning, you find you're too weary to follow through on all those consequences you'd mentally envisioned the night before.

Sound familiar?

One thing every parent knows for sure is that teens make mistakes. But then again, so do we. Sometimes we let our emotions get the best of us, causing us to dole out consequences in the heat of the moment and overreact in a big way. Sometimes we're just so sick and tired of the whole "parenting a teen" gig that we throw our hands up and fail to follow through at all.

I get it, and I've certainly been guilty of overreacting myself. So whether you find yourself at the end of your rope due to that D minus (in Gym? REALLY?!) or because your car was returned to the garage with nothing left in its tank but fumes and optimism, you need a new way of dealing with these frustrating—and yet totally predictable—conflicts.

Behold! A simple strategy that can radically transform your relationships, your home, and your sanity: house rules.*

Sound intimidating and legalistic? Fear not. Creating house rules simply means putting together a document that details your values and expectations as a family. And if your teenager wants privileges—which, according to Merriam Webster, are special rights or advantages—like later curfews, or access to the family vehicle, or a cell phone, they need to abide by the house rules.

House rules are effective because they take the pressure and emotion out of following through on logical consequences. Since both you and your teen agree to the terms ahead of time, they know they have no one to blame but themselves if they screw up.**

If you're dealing with frustrating power struggles with your teen, if you're tired of yelling, if you're sick of ineffective lectures, you should try this. Here's how to get started.

Your Goal

To create and implement well-constructed, clearly defined house rules that will help teens make wise decisions with or without your physical presence.

---

* What? Something that will accomplish all that? What kind of sorcery is this?
** "If" they screw up?! Who are we kidding? More like "when."

What to Expect

CREATE HOUSE RULES DURING A TIME OF PEACE, NOT WAR.

The time to sit down and calmly, rationally discuss hopes, dreams, rules, and consequences is not five minutes after a shouting match. If cooler heads are going to prevail, you and your teen both need to have cool heads to start.

If you sit down with your teen to discuss the house rules and it blows up, don't panic. Instead, give them two options. Say something to this effect: "It seems as if this is the best time for us to do this. So, we have two options: We can push through and get this done today, or we can postpone until tomorrow. I'm going to leave that choice up to you. But we do need to do this. What would you prefer?"

HOUSE RULES MUST BE WRITTEN TOGETHER.

The beauty of house rules is that they work because two different parties agree upon a common course of action. The key phrase here is "agree upon." This should be a productive conversation between you and your teen.

YOU'LL HAVE TO BE INTENTIONAL TO MAKE THIS HAPPEN.

Believe it or not, time is often the biggest hurdle in putting together house rules. Between school, sports, and social events, your teen is probably even busier than you are. And sitting down for a family meeting may sound about as appealing to him as shoveling up the family dog's droppings.

So, try to make it fun. You can hammer out your family's house rules at your favorite restaurant, or sandwich it in between two fun events (ice cream and a shopping trip). But whatever you do, put it on the calendar, and make it a nonnegotiable. This is important stuff.

Are you afraid your teen might balk at the idea of a parent meeting? Truthfully, he might. Try saying something like this to take the pressure off:

"Listen, I know you don't want me to nag you all the time, and I don't want that, either. I've got an idea that will help you do more of the stuff you want to, while I make sure you're taking care of the stuff you need to. Let's sit down together and hammer out a few of the fun things that are most important to you, and then I'll let you know what you need to do to make those things happen. After that, we'll both have a better idea of what we expect from each other."

What to Do

1. **Review the House Rules Template provided below.** I've sketched out the big pieces to get you started. Of course, this is your family and your kid—so edit the house rules as needed to make them your own.

2. **Find out what privileges your teen wants, listen carefully, and negotiate.** Start by asking your teen what privileges she wants to include in the house rules. Listen closely without reacting—even if you think the request is ridiculous. Remember, every day that passes brings your teen that much closer to adulthood. You want her to have privileges and freedoms, because that will help her practice for independence and grow in self-governance.

Once your teen has shared his or her requests, it's time to negotiate. Your teen might want to be allowed to stay out until 3 A.M. every night, but that doesn't mean you're obligated to work that into the contract. Compromise, but hold firm on the nonnegotiables. You are the parent, after all.

3. **Sketch out the rules and consequences.** Now it's your turn. Take a few minutes to review the rules you have for your teen, and the privileges she'll lose if she doesn't follow through. Make sure that the pun-

ishment fits the crime. Remember, this is a road map that tells your teen exactly what she has to do to earn the privileges and freedoms she wants.

4. **Write it all out and have everyone sign the document.** Write out the house rules and sign them together. Verbal contracts are fine for buying things at garage sales, but with something this important, you want to clearly spell things out. And if there are questions or disagreements later, you can simply review the document instead of arguing about what you think you said or what your teen thinks you meant. By signing the house rules, every family member is agreeing to the terms.

Note: If you are coparenting, do everything in your power to get the other parent to agree to one set of rules, privileges, and consequences. One set of house rules should apply, regardless of which house your teen is at. This consistency will be helpful for all parties involved, including your teen.

5. **Follow through.** The most crucial part of the house rules? Following through. Luckily, the prewritten, predetermined document makes that a bit easier. When your teen fails to meet an expectation, the document is there to tell you exactly what to do. Refer to it often, and when it's time to enact a consequence, simply remind (and show) your teen what he agreed to and why he will be losing a privilege. You can also remind him what he needs to do to earn that privilege back. The real beauty of this is that you are no longer the "Bad Guy."

As the adult, you must stick to the rules, just as you expect your teen to do. It's not fair to add on additional punishments because you're upset—let the document do the work for you, and kindly, but firmly, remind your teen of what was agreed upon.

Warning: There will be times when your teen won't be happy with you. Even if you're following the house rules exactly, your teen isn't going to like it when she breaks the agreement and loses a privilege. Expect a reaction, and just remember that even if she's angry, her logical side knows you're right.

HOUSE RULES TEMPLATE

Here's a basic template from which to start developing your house rules.* Feel free to edit the rules as needed to make them your own, so that they work for you and your teen.

Privileges

CAR OR TRANSPORTATION

I can use the family car to drive to my friends' houses, school, and other places I need or want to go, or I can ask my parents to drive me (as long as they aren't busy and don't play embarrassing music).

CASH

My allowance is $____/week for miscellaneous spending. If I want more money, I can ask to do extra work around the house or find a job in town.

CURFEW

I can stay out until ____ on weekends and ____ during the week.

TECHNOLOGY:
Computer, Tablet, Cell Phone, or Wi-Fi

My parents, because of their never-ending awesomeness, will allow me to have access to a computer, tablet, cell phone, or Wi-Fi as appropriate. I understand this is a privilege and not an inalienable right protected by Article 4 of the US Constitution.

---

*   Visit joshshipp.com/ggtth to download an editable version.

OTHER PRIVILEGES (DISCUSS WITH YOUR TEEN)

_____

_____

_____

_____

_____

_____

_____

Rules

THE PURPOSE OF HOUSE RULES

I understand that even though my parents can be embarrassing, they love me more than anything in the world. I understand that these rules are _not_ a form of punishment. Instead, my parents care about me so much that they created these guidelines to help me become an awesome/respectable adult. **Initial here:** _____

MUTUAL RESPECT

I promise to treat my family with respect. This means no yelling, swearing, or saying anything to them that I wouldn't want to go viral on YouTube. Even when we are upset, mad, or having a heated argument, we will fight _for_ each other, not against each other. **Initial here:** _____

CURFEW PROMPTNESS

Because my parents don't want to find me in a ditch or learn that I was abducted by aliens, I'll be home (in the door!) by _____ on weekends and _____ during the week. I will plan for situations and circumstances that might make me late. And I will quickly communicate with my parents if something reasonably unexpected happens. **Initial here:** _____

HELPING OUT

If my parents ask me to help out, I'll do it. Additionally, I will look for ways to help out—even if the task isn't my responsibility. Not because it's my job, but because (1) I want to show them how thankful I am for everything they do for me, and (2) it's proof that I'm basically a ninja and can tackle any challenge. **Initial here:** _____

RADICAL HONESTY

I promise to never lie to my parents, even if I'm embarrassed or afraid to admit a mistake. Even though their high school hairstyles suggest otherwise, they're not dummies and they will know if I'm lying anyway. Additionally, I understand that if I'm ever in a situation that feels unsafe or simply uncomfortable, I can always text the code word _____ to my parents. My parents will pick me up, and I can tell them as much or as little as I want. I understand my parents will never judge me for asking for help. **Initial here:** _____

ACADEMIC EFFORT

Because I want to have an awesome job and not live in the basement forever, I understand that my parents expect me to maintain at least a _____ grade point average in school. I promise to try my best, ask for help when I need it, and not beat myself up if I get a less-than-stellar grade. Working hard makes me and my parents proud. **Initial here:** _____

TECHNOLOGY USE

Technology is an incredible tool that helps me learn about the world, connect with friends, and even order late-night pizza. I understand that my behavior on these devices can directly impact my reputation and future, so I promise to use technology responsibly. In our family, that means _____ and _____ . Lastly, I will exercise intentional restraint and not let technology interfere with my important relationships or obligations. **Initial here:** _____

NO DRUGS OR ALCOHOL

Because I respect myself, I will say "no" to alcohol and drugs and "yes" to safe, fun adventures with my friends and family. Because both drugs and alcohol can severely hurt me and my future, I will choose not to use them. My parents are not trying to rob me of a good time, but they want me to realize my full potential and not end up in legal trouble, jail, or a body bag. **Initial here:** _____

HAVE FUN

Although my parents are sometimes totally lame and pretty embarrassing, I know that they love me and want the best for me. My relationship with them will last the rest of my life. I commit to having fun with my family and seeing the best in them and myself. **Initial here:** _____

OTHER RULES (DISCUSS WITH YOUR TEEN)

_____

_____

_____

_____

Consequences

I understand that if I choose to disregard any of the above rules, there will be consequences. It's not because my parents are jerks, but because they want to help me become a respectable adult.

THE FIRST TIME I BREAK A HOUSE RULE,

I will lose ONE privilege for _____ or until I _____.

                     (period of time)   (way to earn privilege back)

IF I BREAK THE SAME HOUSE RULE AGAIN,

I will lose TWO privileges for _____ or until I _____.

                     (period of time)   (way to earn privilege back)

IF I BREAK THE SAME HOUSE RULE A THIRD TIME,

I will lose ALL privileges for _____ or until I _____ .

(period of time)   (way to earn privilege back)

IF I BREAK THE SAME HOUSE RULE A FOURTH TIME OR IF THE ACTION IS UNLAWFUL:

Because of the severity of this infraction, and the potential (or imminent) harm this could cause to myself and/or others, we will seek the help of a local mental health care professional together for the benefit of the entire family.

I have read this document and agree to the above rules and consequences. I know that my parents created these rules out of love, and I understand that if I have any questions, I should talk to them.

_____

Teen Signature

_____

Parent(s) Signature

How to Improve Communication with Your Teen

The Challenge

Though their eye-rolling and sighing might seem to send strong messages to the contrary, teenagers again and again say that what they want most is more connection with their parents. But how can one do this? What follows is a simple technique that can noticeably improve communication between you and your teen. It's not complex—all it takes is a notebook. In this notebook, you will write longhand notes and letters to each other. You can follow our prompts or make up your own. In the process, you'll find yourselves (hopefully!) asking good questions, responding honestly, and thinking deeply. Because for some reason, parents and teenagers are both able to write things in notebooks more easily than they're able to say them out loud.

Your Goal

To intentionally create a conduit that will improve meaningful communication between you and your teen.

What to Expect

It might be weird at first. As twenty-first-century adult humans, we don't write letters on paper to one another much. It takes awhile to move your hand to form letters with the goose quill. And you might not know exactly what to say.

This isn't going to be easy, but you're going to have to push through that. You might have grown into the habit of not communicating. We also understand that you are an adult and have a myriad of responsibilities. While you are doing this, your mind might start thinking about the two hundred other things that you still need to do. It's okay. This is important. This is going to take intentional effort on your part. If you recall the YMCA teen and parent survey mentioned earlier, teenagers really, truly want to be closer with their parents. But this isn't just going to happen magically on its own. We can do a better job of stepping forward to help open some lines of communication that will improve the relationship.

What to Do

1. **Buy a notebook.** It can be college-ruled. It can have no lines. It can have a fancy cover. It can be a simple hundred-page, wide-ruled composition book. Whatever you like. That's not the important part: What's important is what you write inside.

2. **Write an opening explanatory note to your teen about this notebook and its purpose (see sample note below).** Then choose from the list of discussion questions located at the end of this section. Remember, the goal of the notebook is to open the doors of communication and to ask good questions. It's not to chide or scold your teen, or to express disapproval. It's to be vulnerable and build connection.

3. **Leave this notebook on your teen's bed** (or if the bed appears to be a federal disaster area, leave it somewhere conspicuous with a Post-it on it that reads, "To: _____ From: _____ [Mom/Dad/Other Caring Adult]"*).

---

* Or if you're superhip, a Post-it that says, "Yo. Read this thang."

EXAMPLE OPENING NOTE FROM PARENT

Dear _____,

Someone asked me the other day what the best part of being a dad was. That was easy for me. The best part of being a dad is that I get to be the dad to you. I am very grateful that I get to be your dad. It's like getting a front-row seat to awesome. Not only are you my favorite teenager, but you're one of my favorite people.

I also know that these next few years of high school are probably going to be challenging. I read a statistic the other day that said that teenagers talk to their parents a little less than twelve minutes a day. I thought about that for a while, and it made me really sad.

I also know that relationships are two-way streets, and many of the parents that I know say that they don't have very good communication with their teens. When I was growing up, you know that my relationship with my parents was just okay. Which is fine. But I don't want that to be us. I'd like to try to do better than just okay.

I also know that sometimes it's easier to write things down than say them. Well, it's easier for me, anyway.

So that's why I bought this notebook.

This is our notebook. To write to each other.

Here's how it will work. I will write you a note in the notebook, and I will leave the notebook on your pillow. At the end of the note, I will ask you a question. It can be something I want to know about you. Or something that's interesting to me. Or just something I've always wondered about. For example, I might ask you:

What is your favorite movie? Why?
Write about a song that's really important to you. Why does it mean so much to you?
What is the most important possession you own?
What is your favorite memory from your childhood?

What is the one thing you worry most about right now?
What is the toughest thing you've gone through?

Then you can write me back. You can share with me whatever you want. And at the end of your note, you can ask me a question, and then put the notebook on my pillow. We'll go back and forth.
    I think this will help us communicate better.
    Also, I want you to know that I love you.

Sample Notebook Starter Questions

QUESTIONS FOR PARENTS AND/OR TEENS

- If you had to give every human being one quality, what would it be and why?
- What is the meanest thing someone has ever said to you?
- If you could be a famous athlete, actor, writer, or musician, which would you choose and why?
- If you were invisible, where would you go and what would you do?
- If you had to make a playlist with the best songs you've ever heard in your life, what songs would be on that playlist?
- What is the greatest song ever written? Why?
- What is the most important quality for a boss to have?
- If you could know one thing about the future, what would it be?
- What do you think is the biggest problem in the United States and why?
- What is the most beautiful place (geographically) that you've ever seen?
- Who is the worst teacher you have ever had? What made him or her so awful?

- Read the headlines for today. What news did you find that most upset or confused you?

TEEN QUESTIONS FOR PARENTS

- What was the toughest thing about your childhood?
- What is a treasured moment from your childhood?
- Who was your best friend when you were my age? What did you do together? Why were you best friends?
- What was something dumb you did when you were my age? What did you learn from that experience?
- Do you have any regrets? Do you wish you could have a "do-over" for something in your life?
- How was your relationship with your mom when you were my age?
- What was your favorite memory with your mom when you were my age?
- How was your relationship with your dad when you were my age?
- What was your favorite memory with your dad when you were my age?
- In what ways do you think it's more difficult to be a teenager in today's world compared to when you were growing up?
- When you were my age, did you ever feel lonely or left out? What did you do?

PARENT QUESTIONS FOR TEENS

- Who was your favorite teacher? Why did you like them so much?
- What is something you like about yourself?
- What is one of your earliest memories?
- What's the most difficult thing about being you right now?

- What's the thing you worry about the most right now? (Be honest!)
- What's something you do when you're stressed or upset that seems to help?
- Talk about the time in your life when you felt the most anger. What was going on? Looking back on it, why were you so angry? How did things turn out?
- Talk about the time in your life when you were the most scared. What was going on? Looking back on it, why were you so scared? How did things turn out?
- What's the kindest thing someone has ever said to you?
- Who would you say is your best friend right now? Why do you think he or she is your best friend?

DIFFICULT AND AWKWARD CONVERSATIONS

FADE IN: *EXT. HOUSE—LATE AFTERNOON A nondescript suburban house.*

DISSOLVE TO: *INT. HOUSE, SAMANTHA'S BEDROOM*
SAMANTHA, a fifteen-year-old teenager, sits on top of the striped comforter on her bed with a chemistry book and notes spread out before her. She fidgets with a pencil as she holds her lab notebook. She has earbuds in and is listening to music.

DISSOLVE TO: *INT. HOUSE, STAIRWELL*
ANDREW, the salt-and-pepper-haired, forty-two-year-old father of Samantha, pauses on the stairs. He looks nauseated, grabs the banister, and doubles over. He coughs, sighs, then looks to the sky and wipes his brow. He labors to take the last three steps to the top of the stairs. He stands outside his daughter's bedroom door. He summons up the courage to knock.

DISSOLVE TO: *INT., SAMANTHA'S BEDROOM*

ANDREW: Hey, sweetie.

SAMANTHA: (*Taking earbuds out, a bit confused*) Hey, Dad . . .

ANDREW: (*Sitting awkwardly on bed, crossing legs, then uncrossing them, then crossing them again*) Listen. Uh. I have something I need to talk to you about.

SAMANTHA: (*Picking up on her father's nervous cues*) Is everything all right?

ANDREW: (*Almost crying*) No. (*Catching himself*) Yes. You see, honey, things are . . . um . . . changing. (*He awkwardly sweeps his hand like a presidential candidate*)

SAMANTHA: (*Puzzled*) What's changing?

ANDREW: You see, there comes a time in every young woman's life . . . when . . . things . . .

SAMANTHA: (*Looks suspiciously at her dad*)

ANDREW: (*Changing tactics*) Flowers have to bloom . . .

SAMANTHA: Huh?

ANDREW: . . . but not too soon, because premature blooming. There's frost. And that kills.

SAMANTHA: Oooookay . . .

ANDREW: SEX! Sex is . . . something . . . you need to. Know.

SAMANTHA: (*She realizes what is happening*) Oh my God.

ANDREW: (*Loud exhale, as if in incredible pain*)

SAMANTHA: Are you trying to have the sex talk with me right now?

ANDREW: Yes. It's time you found out.

SAMANTHA: This is really happening, isn't it?

ANDREW: (*Getting up and walking to the dresser*) You see, Sam. When a man and a woman love each other, there's a special hug . . .

SAMANTHA: Dear God.

ANDREW: Like with your mother and me.

SAMANTHA: No. Please. Stop.

ANDREW: Maybe you have questions. About. (*Pauses . . . can't bring himself to say it*) INTERCOURSE!

SAMANTHA: Are you using my Beanie Babies as props?

ANDREW: (*Notices that he's absentmindedly picked up two Beanie Babies. He throws them down quickly.*) No!

SAMANTHA: I don't know if those can be in my room anymore.

ANDREW: Also, condoms don't always work. Your brother is proof of that.

SAMANTHA: (*Shell-shocked*) I . . . I . . . didn't need to know that.

ANDREW: (*Remembering*) I have these books! These are from the library. And this DVD.

SAMANTHA: This is from PBS.

ANDREW: Very informative.

SAMANTHA: I can't believe this is my life right now.

ANDREW: Oh, okay. So. I think this went well. I'll leave you these . . . resources. Also, it's coolest to wait until you're married.

SAMANTHA: Okay.

ANDREW: Okay, well, good talk. So. To recap. Sex. And. Uh. Sexuality. We'll see you later. And I love you.

SAMANTHA: I.

ANDREW: Oh, if you can just sign this sheet. So I can show your mother that we did, indeed, have The Talk.

SAMANTHA: (*Signs the sheet*) Please go.

ANDREW: (*Growing in confidence*) Okay, I think we can both agree that this conversation was so effective, we never need to talk about that subject ever again. Ever.

SAMANTHA: Agreed.

ANDREW: (*Going to door*) Okay, well. Bye.

(*Opens door, hastily closes it behind him*)

DISSOLVE TO: *INT., HOUSE HALLWAY*

ANDREW: (*Falls back against door in relief*)

NARRATOR: There comes a time in every parent's life when you will need to have a difficult or awkward conversation with your teen. This section will help you navigate through those topics so that you won't do what Andrew just did.

ANDREW: (*Smiles, begins to walk down hallway*) Nailed it.

How to Talk to Your Teen About Sex

S pecial thanks to Dr. Jim Burns, executive director of HomeWord Center for Youth and Family at Azusa Pacific University, who was consulted to address the nuances of this topic.

The Challenge

When parents are asked the question "How healthy and open is the dialogue with your teen about sex?" nearly all parents say something like, "Oh, we're good. We have talked about this. My teen clearly knows my values." And nearly all the teens say, "The subject is taboo and we hardly ever talk about it."

The bottom line is this: Teens want and need adult guidance on the topic of sex, but adults tend to clam up, often because this part of parenting was never modeled to them when they were teens.

And also because—dear God.

Although sex is an excruciatingly uncomfortable topic, teens are desperate for information to help them navigate their sexuality, and unless adults guide them, teens are going to get that guidance from unreliable sources: the Internet, popular culture, the media, and their friends.

Your Goal

To help your teens put boundaries and context around the confusing and complex arena of their own sexuality.

What to Expect

The time to have "the talk" is now. It's never too early to start talking about sex with your kid, but the ideal time is usually around ages ten to eleven. At that age, preteens are less influenced by society and their peers. They don't know enough about sex to be embarrassed by it and to know that it's a taboo subject. Once teens start going through puberty, they think differently and are far more likely to be embarrassed by their bodies. And by the time teens hit high school, they are already immersed in our highly sexualized culture, are pulling away developmentally, and are beginning to seek information and resources away from the home.

One of the biggest parenting clichés and myths is about having the dreaded talk. It's not the talk. It's the talks. You can't have just one talk with your teen. One eight-to-fourteen-minute lecture with charts is not enough information for your teen to navigate through adolescence. Nearly all teens say they wish there was more of an ongoing conversation about sex with their parents.[*]

Understand that sex questions are relationship questions. Don't separate sexuality from relationships. As teens approach adulthood, they are endlessly curious about this topic. How do you treat the opposite sex? What does a healthy relationship look like? What should I look for? What are some healthy models? And what are the most

---

[*] Nearly all parents say they'd rather hire Gary Busey as their life coach.

important aspects to a healthy relationship? Have conversations about that.

Because of the vast amount of misinformation out there, teens are left with many questions swirling in their heads and no safe or reliable guides or spaces to ask these questions. The subject of sex is important, and you must figure out a way to begin this dialogue with your teen. One warning: The questions your teen has are often very specific. And that will likely make you uncomfortable. Here's an example. In a recent survey, eight out of ten teen boys said they want to talk about the subject of masturbation, but aren't. At the end of this section, there's a prep sheet with sixteen common teenage questions about sex that you'll need to have the answers to as you begin these conversations.

What to Do

1. **Focus on their questions.** Your goal here is to start and maintain a dialogue (not a monologue). Your tendency will be to lecture and make the conversation one-sided because it's awkward as all get-out. You must resist this tendency, because teens shut down when adults turn preachy and the conversation is one-sided. Teens have questions. Listen and ask questions yourself to figure out their questions and concerns.

2. **Use external examples to gather intelligence.** Some teens are reluctant to discuss sex as it relates to themselves with their parent, but they are perfectly fine talking about other people. Teens are often eager to talk about their friends, and they love to talk about media. These things are external to your teen, and the psychological distance makes these the safest examples. Try these questions: What kinds of relationships are you seeing at school? Are people dating at your school? Do you hear people talking about having sex? What do you think about that? Did you see that thing on TV? What about that news story? What did you think about that?

3. **Watch your tone and emotion.** Remember that your strong opinions can drown out your child's voice. We understand that this is a charged topic, and parents have the right to say what they feel and the obligation to clarify their most important values around this issue. But you must (must!) be careful with your tone. As you begin to have a dialogue with your teen about sexuality, there's a good chance you will discover he or she has different ideas or values than you do around this important issue. This can cause parents to spike with emotion. Be careful here. You cannot force your teen into believing and embracing your values. If your tone is rigid or shaming, you will lose influence with your teen. You have to try different tactics.

4. **Show them a way toward beauty and health.** You know that sexuality that is misused or abused can cause tremendous damage to a person. And so the conversation about sex can sometimes take a decidedly negative turn. But teens also need to know what the good things are about our sexuality. There are some beautiful and important things to say about human sexuality and the good things that can come of it. We're born sexual. We are sexual our whole lives. It's important to help teens put this aspect of their lives into a healthy context.

5. **Be vulnerable, but don't overshare.** You might be wondering, "How much should I share about my own sexual past with my teen?" Make sure to keep the emphasis on your teen and your desire for him or her to make healthy and wise decisions, even if you did not. What do you wish someone had told you about sexuality when you were younger? If your sexual past is not something you'd want to do over, a good line is "I want you to make better choices about this than I did."

Prep Sheet: Sixteen Questions Your Teen Might Have About Sex

The following is a list of sixteen questions on the topic of sex frequently asked by actual teenagers—which means it's highly likely that your teen is thinking about this stuff, too.

Step 1 of 2: Review these questions and determine what your opinions and values are about each one before talking with your teen.

1. How far is too far?
2. When it is okay to have sex? At what age? How do you know when it's okay?
3. Is it possible to get the pill without your parents knowing?
4. How often do married people usually have sexual intercourse?
5. Is oral sex okay?
6. How do girls masturbate?
7. How do boys masturbate?
8. At what age do boys have their first erection?
9. When is a girl most likely to get pregnant? Is the pill expensive? Is the pill dangerous?
10. What are examples of STDs, and how does a person get one?
11. I'm afraid of AIDS. What can I do so as not to get it?
12. If you participate in oral sex, are you still a virgin?
13. What can a guy do if he feels lust toward other guys? How do you handle it?
14. If someone has been sexually abused and hasn't told anyone about it, how can someone try to deal with it?
15. Is it immoral or wrong to have premarital sex?
16. Is it immoral or wrong to have an abortion? What should you do if you know someone who has had one?

Step 2 of 2: Make a copy of the teen survey sheet that follows, and give it to your teen. Have them circle the questions that most resonate with them.

The following is a list of sixteen questions about sex that teenagers frequently ask, which means it's highly likely that you have wondered about some of this stuff, too. Read the questions below and then circle the ones that stand out to you. Don't worry: I won't judge you. And I'll keep this private and just between us.

1. How far is too far?

2. When it is okay to have sex? At what age? How do you know when it's okay?

3. Is it possible to get the pill without your parents knowing?

4. How often do married people usually have sexual intercourse?

5. Is oral sex okay?

6. How do girls masturbate?

7. How do boys masturbate?

8. At what age do boys have their first erection?

9. When is a girl most likely to get pregnant? Is the pill expensive? Is the pill dangerous?

10. What are examples of STDs and how does a person get one?

11. I'm afraid of AIDS. What can I do not to get it?

12. If you participate in oral sex, are you still a virgin?

13. What can a guy do if he feels lust toward other guys? How do you handle it?

14. If someone has been sexually abused and hasn't told anyone about it, how can someone try to deal with it?

15. Is it wrong to have premarital sex?

16. Is it wrong to have an abortion? What should you do if you know someone who has had one?

Okay, So Now What?

Now that your teen has taken the survey, it's time to have a highly awkward yet highly important conversation about sexuality.

Prepare. Look at the questions that your teen circled. This is a test you know the questions to in advance. First, think back to when you were fourteen years old. The key here is a combination of empathy ("I understand what you're going through") and perspective ("Here's what I wish someone had told me"). Your kids don't need (or want!) details, but they do want honesty about how you arrived at your values on sex.

Pick a time and a place that works to your advantage. Have this chat when just you and your teen will be in the car together for fifteen or more minutes. The car provides the perfect trifecta for having awkward conversations: It's informal, it doesn't require eye contact, and you're locked in a vehicle moving 65 miles per hour.

To start, limit yourself to ONE question that your teen circled. The goal here is to have this quick chat go well, so your teen won't be adamantly opposed to talking with you about this again. So your objective is one question, one win, and then stop. You'll want to keep going. You'll be tempted to address all the questions. Don't. Bask in the small victory and realize you've gained permission for future chats.

How to Talk to Your Teen About Death

Special thanks to Dr. Kimberly Allen, associate professor in the Department of Youth, Family, and Community Sciences at North Carolina State University, who was consulted to address the nuances of this topic.

The Challenge

Dealing with death, especially a sudden or tragic death, is something I hope you and your teen don't ever have to face. But unfortunately you probably will. It's highly unlikely your teenager will graduate from high school without attending at least one funeral.

As I was writing these words, my friend texted me. A dad at his kid's school suddenly and shockingly passed away. The entire school community is devastated. And that man's wife and two kids are left with a tragedy every morning when they wake up and he isn't there. His daughter keeps setting a place at the dinner table for her daddy. The emptiness of that seat causes a pain for that family that I can't even imagine.

Often, the sheer emotional trauma of this kind of event can leave even the strongest adult feeling helpless and confused. Here are some best practices that we hope will help not only your teen but also you get through.

Your Goal

To help your teen through the grief process as skillfully and compassionately as possible.

What to Expect

1. **There is no such thing as normal.** I was at a local high school recently where a student had tragically died. The faculty, all of whom truly cared about the teens in the classes, were divided on how to best operate as teachers. Some faculty members suggested that things continue as normal. "Our teens need us to be consistent and solid for them," they said. "This helps them feel that things will go back to normal, that not everything is changing." Other teachers felt that there were kids who simply wouldn't be able to function like that. They wanted to shut down class in order to give the students space to talk and cry. The point is, both sides were right. There's no one way that kids process grief. Some kids need business as usual. And for other kids, there's no way they're going to be okay with that. Some kids want to talk right away. Other teens have a delayed emotional reaction and don't grieve for a week or two. Ask your teens what they think they need. Pay attention. And remember that there's no wrong or right way.

2. **Feelings of helplessness.** Perhaps the worst thing about facing a death is that you feel out of control psychologically. This is natural both for you and for your teen. Your goal is to help teens deal with those feelings of helplessness and empower them. You want to help them see that not all of life is spinning wildly out of control.

3. **Potential volatility.** Think about your teenager like a balloon. The incredible stress of death and all the emotions it causes can fill teens up with negative emotions to the point where they are overinflated. Our bodies literally can't handle that kind of stress, just can't hold it all in. Sometimes teens pop. This might come out as jerky, disrespectful behavior, but it is likely the result of grief and psychological distress.

As an adult, you simply must be your kindest, most patient, most loving self.

4. **Questions you won't be able to answer.** If something tragic happens, like the sudden death of a classmate, your teen will be wildly searching for answers as to why it happened. You might be, too. Unfortunately, these answers hardly ever appear, and searching for them will hardly ever lead to satisfaction. Sometimes the best thing you can say is "I don't know why this has happened. But I'm very sad about it, too."

What to Do

1. **Make yourself available.** There's an old Jewish practice called sitting shiva. The word "shiva" simply means seven. Immediately after a death, friends and loved ones go to the mourner's home and sit quietly for seven days. The protocol is that you are not supposed to say anything until and unless the person mourning initiates a conversation. The goal is simply to let the person mourning know that you are there and are willing to talk if the other person needs to. The best thing you can do for a teenager in the wake of death is to sit shiva: Make yourself available. This is especially important right after a loss. A helpful line you can use is "I'm here if you want to talk." And then make sure you are actually available.

2. **Never direct your teen on how to grieve.** Many well-meaning adults make mistakes in one of two ways. First, they will advise their teens to "try not to think about it." This is never helpful. It wouldn't be helpful if someone said it to you, would it? Second, sometimes well-meaning adults try to force teens to talk, saying something like "Come on. You need to talk to me." Sure, it's very good to talk these things out. But forcing teens to talk when they aren't ready can also be destructive. Again, an effective line to use is "I'm here if you want to talk." You can say this same line to your teen periodically (or via text) as a gentle reminder that you are available to talk whenever he or she is ready.

3. **Pay attention to what your teen needs.** Because the grief process varies so much from teen to teen, it's good to be sensitive to what your particular teen needs. Some teens need space. Some teens need to distract themselves. Teens often have an instinctive sense of what they need, but sometimes adults have to weigh what the teen is saying against what we know to be true of them. Teens might need to stay home from school for a while, but eventually they have to get back to a normal routine. The point is to involve them in this conversation. Be available to help them make decisions. Think about what you need and what's reasonable.

4. **Help your teen grieve by telling his or her story.** One of the things we know about grief and trauma is that it produces strong feelings of helplessness. We also know that teens feel more in control and safer when they are able to tell the story about what happened and how it affected them. Telling our stories is a huge aspect of human grieving. And from a physiological perspective, as teens are able to process what happened, it frees the body of stress hormones. This is where artistic expression such as journaling, music, and art can really help. These activities allow teens to think deeply about what happened and how it affected them, and share those thoughts.

5. **Pay attention to red flags.** Here are some potential signs that your teen is having a particularly difficult time processing death and likely needs some extra help to get through this period. If you see any of these red flags, please seek help from a qualified counselor.

- If your teen begins isolating himself or herself from other people and refusing to interact, even with friends.
- If there is evidence of insomnia or sleeplessness.
- If there is a long period of silence or a strict refusal to talk.
- If your teen begins repeatedly saying things like "I can't take this."
- If your teen's performance in school begins to drop in uncharacteristic ways.
- If you see your teen using negative coping techniques for the purpose of escaping (drug or alcohol abuse, withdrawal from the real world, and so forth).

How to Convince Your Teen to Get Help

Special thanks to Dr. Jerry Weichman, a clinical psychologist, adolescent specialist, and founder of the Weichman Clinic, an innovative counseling and treatment center for children and teens, who was consulted to address the nuances of this topic.

The Challenge

What you don't talk out, you act out. Counselors help people (especially teens) talk things out. They also help you understand yourself. For teenagers, rapidly changing and complex humans who sometimes can't understand themselves, this is a gift.

So how do you know when a teen should get counseling? Are there particular situations or scenarios to look for? The short answer is yes. In 1967, psychiatrists Thomas Holmes and Richard Rahe examined the medical records of over five thousand medical patients to try to determine whether stressful life events might cause illnesses. They found that these events did. Holmes and Rahe rated a series of life events and assigned "stress scores" to each event. The higher the score (on a scale of 1–100), the more stressful the event. Here's a list of the some of the life events relevant to teens and their relative stress scores:

Divorce of parents (73), parents separating (65), death of a family member (63), serious personal illness (53), serious illness of a family member (44), sexual difficulties (39), parent loses job/large financial change (38), death of a friend (37), sibling leaving home (29), move houses (25), trouble with teacher or coach (23), change of school (20), change of social circles (20).

If any of these events (or an unfortunate combination of these events) happen in the life of your teen, it can cause your teen's stress score to climb, and he or she may not be able to cope with the stress. In the end, though, trust your gut. If you're paying attention and feel that something is "off" with your teen, press in and consider counseling.

Counselors help you deal with your hurt. Who you think you are affects the choices that you make, and the choices you make affect your future. Counseling helps you more clearly see who you are and what you are capable of. My counselors have helped me see past the lies that I've believed about myself. They've helped me sort through the garbage in my past and my own hurt.

As my friend Jon Acuff, an author and speaker, says, "The best time to see a counselor is before you need one. Don't wait for a fire to invest in a smoke alarm." Sound advice, Jon.

Your Goal

To remove the stigma around counseling and persuade your teen to give counseling a chance.

What to Expect

1. **Preconceived stigmas about counseling.** For many teens, the second you say, "I think it might be a good idea for you to get some counseling," they hear "I think you're a screwed-up, horrible human being."

Teens are already swirling with insecurity and fear, and when the topic of counseling is brought up, it can trigger feelings of shame. Dr. Brené Brown, a bestselling author and research professor at the

University of Houston Graduate College of Social Work, defines shame in this way: "Is there something about me that if other people know it or see it, then I won't be worthy of connection?" If you're going to help your teen, you should keep an eye out for this emotional pitfall when it comes to counseling.

2. **Pushback.** Teens know that counseling will mean talking about themselves and experiences they've had, often painful experiences or aspects of themselves they either don't like or don't understand. This means committing to a level of personal vulnerability so incredibly frightening that most teens would rather run away. Lead with vulnerability and compassion so your teen doesn't "tough guy" it up.

What to Do

1. **Remove the stigma.** Let's all stop and admit this once and for all: Everybody on the planet is a little bit dysfunctional. Myself included.* All of us have challenges—the question is just whether you will face yours.

One great way to remove the stigma with your teen is to be vulnerable about your own need for help. If you have been to a counselor, lead with that information. You can say something like "Counseling isn't for weak people. It's for people who are honest and brave enough to say, 'I really want to understand this and I think I need a guide to help me figure it out.'"

2. **Find a compatible counselor.** Compatibility with a counselor is important. Unfortunately, there's no computer algorithm available to help pair your teen with the perfect counselor and ensure a good match. There are counselors who are a great fit and those who are a

---

* Fun fact: I once threatened to burn all my children's toys because they refused to pick them up. To which my adorable, pigtailed, four-year-old daughter said, "If you do that, Daddy, I will punch you in the penis."

bad fit, and it's not necessarily a knock on the counselor if they aren't the right fit. Some teens need someone who is empathic. Some teens need to be pushed. Some teens need clear strategies.

When doing this, make sure you clearly communicate two key points to your teen:

- **You and I will work together to find a counselor.** That's our end goal.
- **You (the teen) will have complete veto power.** No questions asked.

Following through on these points helps keep the ball rolling and allows your teen a strong sense of power and agency. Consider booking an introductory session with a counselor with the sole purpose of seeing if your teen connects with and trusts that person.

3. **Set healthy expectations from the start.** Counseling is going to suck for the first couple of weeks. You're going to leave feeling worse than when you went in. After you go to the gym, you're often very sore, right? This is a good thing, because the pain is a sign that your intense workout is enabling you to build muscle. The same is true in counseling: The soreness (emotionally) is a sign that the process is working. The best thing you can do is help teens set realistic expectations so that when they leave sessions feeling worse than they did when they went in, they'll see it as a sign that they are making progress.

4. **Give your teen a clear out.** Remember: The goal isn't to get your teen to go to one counseling session. Your goal is for your teen to willingly want to go back. You must give teens an out so they don't feel like they are being forced to do something they don't want to do. Say something like this: "So we've found this counselor, and everyone we've talked to says this person is awesome. Here's my challenge to you: I want you to try just five sessions with Dr. So-and-So. If after five sessions you don't feel your time with the counselor is valuable, you can come to me and say I want out. No questions asked. I won't harass you or give you a hard time." Giving them that out can be the needed motivator to get them there and keep them there.

Choosing an Effective Teen Counselor

1. **Make sure they're licensed.** Mental health professionals are regulated by state boards, much like medical doctors. In order to become licensed, a counselor must undergo formal schooling from an accredited university, and log hundreds of hours of internship and practice. Here are the four main types of counseling professionals you're likely to encounter.

> **Psychologists** have a doctorate in psychology and undergo at least four years of graduate training in research, human behavior, and therapeutic techniques. In addition to conducting therapy, they specialize in the administration of psychological tests and assessments and carry out psychological research.

> **Psychiatrists** are medical doctors. They attend medical school and complete a three- to five-year psychiatric residency. They have the ability to assess the need for and prescribe medication for mental health problems.

> **Social workers** have a master's degree in social work, which entails two years of education and training. A unique characteristic of social workers is their knowledge of social support systems, organizations, and groups and how these affect an individual's psychological well-being.

> **Counselors** have specialized training in particular areas and/or they may have advanced degrees (e.g., master's degrees) in counseling-related fields such as mental health counseling or psychology. They tend to deal with very specific problems, such as alcohol addiction or career indecision.

2. **Find a counselor who is a teen specialist.** You must find a counselor who specializes in working with teenagers. This is important

because a teenager's brain operates in a vastly different way than an adult's brain. Your teen also needs a counselor who has spent enough time with teenagers to know what the common themes and pressures are of that age group. Some questions to ask a potential therapist are: What percentage of your caseload is teens? How long have you been working with teenagers?

3. **Involve your teen.** The single most critical aspect of counseling is the therapeutic relationship between your teen and the therapist. At best you get only one or two shots at putting someone in front of teens who they are going to think is cool and who they want to talk to again. So go in knowing that you don't get too many reloads. And—we know you don't want to hear this—saving money isn't worth losing opportunity. Find someone who has a youthful approach (and ideally, someone who even looks a little younger). You want teens to be open to coming back because the experience was cool for them, or because they feel like that person "got" them. Some questions you might ask your teen are: So, what were your impressions? Did you feel as though he/she understood you? Do you think he/she can help you?

Common Hurdle: "But What If I Don't Have the Money?"

Unfortunately, mental health is one of the least reimbursed forms of health care, especially one-on-one counseling sessions.

Here are a few ways to be resourceful:

- Check to see if it's possible for you to be fully or partially reimbursed by your health care plan.
- Check to see if your teen's school has resources.
- Call local nonprofits and organizations to see if they have funds or counselors who will do pro bono work or sliding-scale (pay-what-you-can) sessions. Assume it will take twenty noes to get one yes.

- Think of counseling as an investment. If you can manage to scrape together the funds, it's far better to do preventive care than some of the more drastic measures that I've seen parents have to take at the other end of the spectrum.
- Get wildly proactive and assemble a collection of caring adults. Contact the school counselor, bring your teen's pediatrician into the fold, call on a stable of caring adults (your teen's favorite uncle, the youth pastor, the local librarian, whomever), and make it a "whole village" effort.

DANGEROUS OR CONCERNING BEHAVIOR

FADE IN: *EXT. HOUSE—LATE AFTERNOON*
A nondescript suburban house.
DISSOLVE TO: *INT. HOUSE, LONG HALLWAY*
DISSOLVE TO: *INT., BEDROOM*
ANDREA, a middle-aged woman with auburn hair, walks with pur-
pose into the room. She pulls the white panel door closed behind her.
There is a look of severity on her face.
DISSOLVE TO:

ANDREA: (*Shutting door*)
DOUG: (*Andrea's husband, looking up from a magazine*) What's
going on?
ANDREA: So I was packing.
DOUG: For science camp?
ANDREA: Right. I needed a bag. And I didn't want to take our
luggage because they have gravel roads up there and it's just too
difficult.
DOUG: Okay.
ANDREA: So I go into Cullen's room to find one of his gym
bags. You know, he's got all those Adidas bags.
DOUG: Yeah?
ANDREA: So I open up his closet, and see one on the floor in

the back of the closet. And I take it to our room and open it up to start packing.

DOUG: And?

ANDREA: I found this. (*Pulls out a small plastic bag filled with green matter and a bong*)

DOUG: Wow. Is that . . .

ANDREA: Yeah.

DOUG: Where did he get this?

ANDREA: Like I know. What are we going to do?

DOUG: I don't know. How did he even get this?

ANDREA: How would I know?

DOUG: (*Musing, and genuinely confused*) I still don't understand. Is this legal, but only if you're eighteen? And do you have to have a card?

ANDREA: I don't know.

DOUG: I think the law changes in January.

ANDREA: That's beside the point, Doug. It's not legal in my house. I don't care what the state says. Our son has drugs! In his room!

DOUG: I mean, you make it sound like you stumbled onto his hidden meth lab. This is a bag of weed.

ANDREA: So?

DOUG: Most kids try drugs and then just move on. It's not that uncommon.

ANDREA: Tammy Smith's son Jeremy.

DOUG: Jeremy died of an overdose of heroin, honey. You can't really die of a marijuana overdose.

ANDREA: Which he was doing because he started with marijuana.

DOUG: I mean . . .

ANDREA: He started doing that (*Pointing to bag*) and then started hanging out with the wrong kids.

DOUG: Most kids . . .

ANDREA: (*With steel in her voice*) Tell that to Tammy Smith. Go ahead. Tell her that. Explain that to her.

DOUG: (*Silent*)

ANDREA: You sat next to me at the funeral. (*Fuming now*) I can't believe I have to fight with you about whether it's okay for our son to possess drugs.

DOUG: (*Relenting*) I'm not arguing with you. I'm not. I just don't know what to do . . . next.

ANDREA: I mean, do we call the police?

DOUG: I don't think they'd bother with an amount this small, babe. I just don't think they would.

ANDREA: Maybe we march down there, pull him out of school, and confront him with everything right there.

DOUG: I wish we had more information.

ANDREA: (*Accusatory, almost sarcastically*) What the hell more information do you need?

DOUG: (*Stiffening: that attack felt unfair*) Look, I'm not the bad guy here. What I mean is, we could be jumping to conclusions. We don't know that the drugs are even his. It could belong to one of his friends. Someone on his team. They could have asked him to hang on to it for him. The point is, we don't know.

ANDREA: So. What now?

DOUG: I don't know.

NARRATOR: There are situations in life where you become aware that your teen in engaging in highly risky, perhaps even dangerous or illegal behavior. This can be paralyzing because the potential outcomes are so severe. But this section can give you the tools to truly help your teen.

Seven Warning Signs Every Parent Must Know

It's entirely possible that your teens will encounter something in their lives that is so burdensome or difficult or complex that they simply won't have the tools to process or deal with it. They likely will need some help from caring adults. The following is a list of critical warning signs that your teen is really struggling and needs help. If you ever become worried that your teen is not okay, come back and review this checklist.

1. **Dramatic changes in sleep.**
   Teen suddenly starts sleeping a lot more (lethargic) or a lot less (insomnia). This can also include trouble falling asleep, trouble going back to sleep after waking up during the night, waking up at all hours of the night, and/or waking up before the alarm clock goes off.
2. **Dramatic changes in eating patterns.**
   Teen suddenly starts eating a great deal more or a lot less.
3. **Sudden difficulty concentrating on anything.**
   Teen always seems to be "someplace else" or shows signs of mental and physical fatigue during the day. Often this is because depression interrupts sleep and that wreaks havoc on teenagers' bodies and brains, but it could also be due to drugs or other forms of self-medication.
4. **A sudden drop in grades.**
   When teenagers are emotionally overwhelmed by life, it is very difficult for them to concentrate and focus in school, and

this may be reflected in their grades and on their report cards. Additionally, this can often cause sleep problems, fatigue, and low energy, which make succeeding in normal, academically demanding environments very difficult.

5. **More irritable than usual.**

Teenagers are often irritable, but other factors can cause a spike in this behavior. For example, teen depression doesn't look the same as adult depression: Hurt and pain can easily turn to anger if it's not properly dealt with. In addition, teens typically don't have the coping strategies that adults do, so a high percentage of teens turn more irritable than usual when they feel overwhelmed by life.

6. **Rapid switch in routine.**

Teens are creatures of habit, so if you notice any dramatic changes in daily routines (when and where they come and go), this could be a warning sign that something is going on. For example, sometimes kids who are bullied suddenly vary their routes and timing. Also, if your teen goes missing on certain nights or turns incredibly hairy during full moons, that could be an indicator that he or she is a werewolf.

7. **Rapid switch in friend groups.**

Although this is not necessarily a sign of trouble, friend groups are a crucial part of a teen's life, and a dramatic change in social circles likely means something important is happening.

I'm Worried My Teen Has an Eating Disorder

Special thanks to Dr. Nicole Siegfried, clinical director at the Highlands Treatment Center for Eating Disorders, who was consulted to address the nuances of this topic.

The Challenge

In 1995, Dr. Anne E. Becker, director of research at the Harvard Eating Disorders Center, took a team of researchers to the remote tropical island of Fiji to interview teenage girls in secondary school.

The researchers were looking for clues into the unique culture of this South Pacific nation, where a robust, nicely rounded body is the norm for men and women. The researchers found that the term "you've gained some weight" was seen as a compliment to the Fijian teens. Calling someone "skinny legs" was an insult, and "going thin"—a term for losing a lot of weight—was cause for concern.

Three years later, the researchers returned and found staggeringly different results. Before 1995, the notion of calories was foreign to the native inhabitants. But by 1998, 69 percent of teenagers said they had been on a diet. Fifteen percent of teenage girls said they had induced vomiting to try to control their weight, and nearly 30 percent of all the girls scored highly on a survey that assessed risk for eating disorders.[7]

What happened? One month after Dr. Becker started her research in 1995, satellites began beaming television signals from the United

States to the Fijian region. The introduction of American television to Fiji's main island, Viti Levu, brought with it vastly different cultural ideas of beauty.[8]

Today in the United States, more than half of teenage girls and nearly a third of teenage boys use unhealthy weight control behaviors such as skipping meals, fasting, smoking cigarettes, vomiting, and taking laxatives. And more than 95 percent of people diagnosed for eating disorders are between the ages of twelve and twenty-five.

While eating disorders and their root causes are nuanced and complex issues, we do know that the teenage years are particularly challenging for eating disorders given the emotional and physical changes, as well as the academic, family, and peer pressures.

Your Goal

Model healthy food habits and create an environment where the focus is on the *internal* traits of teenagers as opposed to their physical appearance.

What to Expect

1. **Confusion.** You're going to have to help your teen navigate how to have a healthy relationship with food. Humans eat food for two main reasons: nourishment and pleasure. It's important to help your teen achieve some sort of balance between "healthy" and "tasty." Because everyone knows that if you eat Cheetos all the time, your hair will turn orange. And if you eat nothing but kale every meal, you will lose your will to live.

2. **Massive Social Pressure.** The explosion of photo-sharing sites places enormous pressure on young people to create a contrived image of physical perfection. Today, more than 90 percent of teens post pictures of themselves online. And after posting, teens often obsess

over the number of likes they receive, because this near-immediate feedback helps validate them. Or doesn't. This modern digital world creates tremendous anxiety and insecurity.

3. **Warning signs.** Be concerned if you hear the word "diet" from your teen. For most parents, the word "diet" seems healthy and benign, but it's actually a high-risk factor for eating disorders. Here's the hard data: 35 percent of "normal dieters" progress to pathological dieting,[9] and of those, 20 to 25 percent progress to partial or full-syndrome eating disorders.[10] Dieting is an attempt by teens to produce a temporary change in their appearance and hardly ever results in long-term healthy behaviors.[11] Any time you hear the phrase "I'm so fat" or "I need to lose weight" or "I need to go on a diet," that should be a yellow flag. Seize that opportunity to begin to talk about food.

What to Do

1. **Be careful with how you talk about food, weight, and appearance.** Teens whose parents talk negatively about their own bodies have a much higher risk for eating disorders. Comments like "I'm so fat" or "It's going to take me a week to burn off this piece of pizza" might seem harmless, but they send cues to kids about what to care about. There's a big difference between "I want to be more active" or "I want to cut out ice cream at night and eat grapes instead" and "I hate the way I look" or "that celebrity sure has let himself go!" The more you talk about issues of physical appearance, the more your teen thinks that value and importance is skin deep.

2. **Focus on what real beauty is.** There will come a time when your teenager will say something like "I'm so ugly" or "I'm fat" or "I'm not pretty," even though most parents go out of their way to try to keep their son or daughter from feeling that way. Part of the role of healthy families is to offset some of the destructive or toxic messages from society. We live in a culture where unrealistic beauty standards are ubiquitous, but the family can be a buffer against what a teen is

seeing and hearing in school or in wider society. Focus on the internal aspects of your teenager's character and why those things make him or her truly beautiful. Here are two strategies to follow:

- **The validate strategy.** Although every parent wishes the words "That's nonsense, you're beautiful" would do the trick, the fact is, they won't. Body image is about one's psychological relationship to one's own body, so affirming teens' feelings and validating their experiences are imperative. Start by saying something like "I heard you say that you feel you're not handsome/pretty. What would make you say that?" Approach the comment with curiosity. Then validate their feelings. Something like "It must be super tough to see all these unrealistic images everywhere you look." Try to use words like "I hear what you're saying" or "I can understand where you're coming from."

- **The combat strategy.** After you validate, you have to directly attack those bad ideas. Say something like "From my end, as your dad/mom, hearing you say that you're ugly, well, that just sounds crazy. That is the furthest thing from the truth. Let me tell you what I see that makes you beautiful." And then list nonphysical traits that make your daughter or son really special and beautiful. Say things like "You have a great sense of humor" or "You're a super loyal and a caring friend" or "I love the way you bring people together" or "I am so impressed by how hard you work at things that are important to you." Don't underestimate your role in helping your teen combat those errors in thinking. Also, make sure to do this regularly—it's impossible to over-validate your teen.

3. **Talk back to the TV.** Your teen will see unhealthy ideas about beauty nearly everywhere. When these ideas appear in your presence, provide real-time running commentary. For example, when that commercial comes on for the new razor, point out that not once in the history of

human shaving has a man shaved and then instantly had a scantily clad female emerge from behind him to check out the smoothness of his shave. Why is the razor company showing this? What are they implying their multiblade razor will do? Talking about this will help teach your teens to be critical consumers of the messages they receive. Do battle with the reigning worldview.

4. **Be vigilant.** The tough thing about eating disorders is that they are, by their very definition, secretive disorders. In fact, on average, people who have eating disorders don't get help until they've been dealing with the issue for five years. But there are things you can pay attention to: If there is a change in a teen's behavior around food. If they suddenly insist on eating dinner only in their room, or they decide to cut out an entire food group. If you find wrappers hidden in their room. If something about their food choices just doesn't add up to you, please press in and investigate. There's a good chance that it's nothing: Teens go through growth spurts and their eating habits can suddenly change. But in this case, it's better to be safe than sorry.

5. **Get professional help.** If you notice any worrisome signs or are concerned that your teen might be struggling with an eating disorder, seek professional help.

I'm Worried My Teen Is Acting Out in Anger

Special thanks to Joshua Wayne, MA, family counselor and director of One Caring Adult, who was consulted to address the nuances of this topic.

The Challenge

Let's be honest—having your teenager behave badly, act defiantly, and speak disrespectfully is enough to push all your buttons and pull all your levers. And if you're not careful, you'll end up yelling back or acting out in anger in response. Maybe you're stuck in that pattern right now.

Remember the core thesis of parenting: One of the most critical things is the strength of your connection with your teen. If you have a strong connection with your teen, and in particular if your teen perceives that he or she is able to be real with you, then—and only then—do you have a chance to influence his or her behavior. Your only real leverage point is your connection to them. This doesn't mean you devolve into an enabling-buddy. It means you use your authority, wisdom, and influence as an adult to connect with and help your teen.

Yelling matches, grounding your teen for a hundred years, and slamming doors won't get that job done. Here's a game plan for not losing your cool and effectively guiding your teen away from bad behavior into maturity while simultaneously not blowing up any relational bridges.

Your Goal

Train your teen that the way to get things from you comes from being respectful and civil.

What to Expect

Every teenager's behavior is almost exclusively influenced by the desire to obtain the four fundamental psychological needs.* You could even say these are four basic needs. And every fight that you have with your teen is them attempting to get one of these four basic needs but doing it in an immature or reckless way. These four needs are:

1. **Love and belonging.** Your teen really wants and needs to feel connected to other people. This connection can come from family and friends, and from groups and organizations they are a part of.

How this plays out: Studies consistently show that teens join gangs to feel a sense of belonging. Now, while this might seem like an improbable choice for your teen, they will "gang up" with anyone who promises belonging. Even if that someone is negative or destructive.

2. **Power.** Your teen needs to feel a sense of accomplishment. This can be from achievement in sports or academics, or simply from having friends they feel good about being around.

How this plays out: They might refuse to clean their room, despite being asked roughly 6,471 times. Why? It's not because they

---

* This idea is called choice theory and was posited by famed psychiatrist Dr. William Glasser in his book by the same name. Glasser outlined these four fundamental psychological needs as the driving force behind nearly all human behavior.

love dwelling in a biohazard zone. It's because they're grasping for power wherever they can and believe they should have authority over their personal space. And their bedroom is their most sacred personal space.

3. **Freedom.** Teens want to have autonomy over parts of their life. This can be by getting a job or a driver's license, or simply by controlling their own schedule.

How this plays out: They might wear clothes you don't like and choose hairstyles you think are hideous. They might argue (vehemently!) against things you believe, just to be contrarian. They are "trying on" different personas in the name of personal freedom.

4. **Fun.** Don't underestimate what a powerful driver of teenager behavior this is: Teenagers are fun addicts. Fun for them can be playing video games, going to movies, or (mostly) hanging out with their friends.

How this plays out: They might do something dumb—like drink at a party or climb into a shopping cart and career down a steep hill—because it sounded fun at the time. The potential consequences are completely overshadowed by the promise of adventure, thrill, or fun.

Again, these four things are good. There is nothing wrong with needing and wanting these things. Every human does. But there is something wrong with throwing tantrums, speaking disrespectfully, and bullying other people to get what you want. Your job is to help coach teens on how to understand what they want and then how to respectfully ask for what they want, modeling civility and love.

What to Do

1. **You need to do some preparation.** During a time of peace (not during a war or an argument), think of the three to five most challenging behaviors you experience with your teen. Now think about

each of these behaviors in terms of the four basic needs. Which of the needs are they most intensely trying to satisfy through these behaviors? How are they going about meeting each need in both positive and negative ways? If you can think this through with someone else (like your spouse), you can exchange ideas and feedback.

2. **Stay calm.** Don't have intense conversations with your teen if you're not calm. And don't have an intense conversation with your teen if he or she is not calm. This is very important. Your teen knows how to push your buttons and how to elicit a response. You must take away your teen's access to your emotional control panel. How do you do this? By being willing to walk away and gain composure.

Consider using a line like the following: "If you want something from me, then let's talk when you are ready to be reasonable and kind to me."

You must stay calm for two main reasons. First, you're going to respond better if you're not driven by your own emotions. Ranting might drive ratings for cable political shows, but it's not effective in real life. And second, whether you realize it or not, you are still the main role model for your teen. You can't tell your teen to stop yelling if you can't stop yelling. If you want your teen to handle emotions with maturity, then you have to be mature.

3. **Teach teens how to get what they want by showing them that their current tactics aren't going to work.** Ask them these questions: What do you want here? What is your goal? What are you trying to get to? And then explain how their behavior won't help their campaign, allowing them to see the big picture. Does your teen throw temper tantrums? Let him know you refuse to engage in conversation until he's speaking calmly. Does your teen ask for things at the very last minute? Let your teen know that you'll be happy to oblige if you are given enough time to plan ahead. Does your teen use disrespectful tones or language? Let her know that the only way she will get what she wants

is to speak with respect to you and others. Again, your teen is almost always aiming for one of the four basic needs listed above; he or she is just behaving badly while trying to get it. When you're both calm, help them see that what they want is fine, but the way they're going about getting it won't result in them getting it.

4. **Utilize the "Kenny Rogers method."** You dramatically weaken your relationship with your teens by chronically fighting a bunch of battles you can't win (and shouldn't even try to). In the immortal words of Kenny Rogers, "You got to know when to hold 'em. Know when to fold 'em. Know when to walk away."

- **Know when to hold 'em.** If you're going to pick and choose your battles, there are times when you simply have to dig in your heels and hold tight. The battles you cannot lose usually revolve around issues of safety and respect. For example, "You cannot talk to people, especially me, that way" or "I need to know where you are at all times" or "You cannot destroy property, including mine." Issues around safety or respect: These are simply nonnegotiables.

- **Know when to fold 'em.** There are some battles in which the more you try to exert your control over teens, the more you will give them reason to push back. Most of these losing battles are over personal autonomy and often are just part of a phase. The number one battle here seems to revolve around teens keeping their room clean. As long as there isn't open food or used food containers piling up in their room (creating a haven for ants) or the smell doesn't seep into the hall, let them keep their room however they want. The same goes for issues of clothes, hairstyle, hair color, and music. Most of the time, teens are just trying things out. These are phase issues, and the more you try to control these behaviors, the more you give them reason to push back.

- **Know when to walk away.** Don't let your kids bully you. If they yell, if they call you names, if they raise their voice or threaten you, you must not capitulate. Instead, say this: "We're not going to have this conversation if you're yelling. When you can behave like the respectful sixteen-year-old that I know you are, then we will have this conversation." And then, walk away. If they attempt to follow you, go into your bedroom and close the door. If they persist, say firmly, "This has to stop now or there will be other consequences."

How to Handle Their Anger: How It Might Play Out

FADE IN: EXT.—LATE SATURDAY MORNING AROUND 11:30 A.M.

A nondescript urban brownstone.

DISSOLVE TO: INT., KITCHEN

MOM is cutting up orange slices and putting them in a large gallon-sized plastic bag.

TEEN, a fifteen-year-old teenage male, enters into the room.

TEEN: Mom. I have to go to Johnny's house.

MOM: Well, your sister has soccer practice, so I have to take her to that.

TEEN: When will you be done?

MOM: We'll be back around three, I imagine.

TEEN: What? That's too long. I need to go to there by noon. That's when everyone is meeting.

MOM: Well, I can take you at three.

TEEN: Mom! I have to go to Johnny's, like, now. I have this project for school and this is the only time Johnny and Angel and them can meet me. So I have to go.

MOM: Well, if you needed to go so badly, you should have told me last night or the night before. I could have planned and made something work.

WHAT YOUR WORDS COMMUNICATE:
Planning is important. This could have ended better for everyone if you had planned.

WHAT THEY'RE DOING:
Your teen will throw in new information to show that this event is indeed an emergency.

TEEN: But I didn't know until, like, right now that everyone was going over there at noon.

MOM: Well, I can't take you, but let's brainstorm. Is there anyone who you could call to get a ride over there? Maybe one of the other moms could swing by and pick you up . . .

WHAT YOUR WORDS COMMUNICATE:
There are times when I can't be your solution, but you're not alone. I will help you brainstorm ways to solve your problem.

TEEN: God! No! That's the whole point! Nobody lives near us.

MOM: Well, I will be back at three.

WHAT YOUR WORDS COMMUNICATE:
Poor planning on your part does not constitute an emergency for everyone else to solve. This is not the way the adult world operates.

TEEN: They need me for the project. I told them I'd be there.

MOM: Well, I'm sorry you did that. I'll be glad to take you, I just can't right now.

WHAT YOUR WORDS COMMUNICATE:

This is key. The phrase "I'll be glad to take you" communicates that you are *for* your teen and want to help them, but this is about give-and-take. Is there a compromise you can make with me? Could you have told me yesterday? Next time what can you do differently? What are some different skills you could use to get what you want?

TEEN: This is bull. I'm stuck here because of her stupid game.

MOM: Look, you can't come to me at the last minute when I'm walking out the door to take your sister to soccer and say you need a ride to Johnny's.

WHAT YOUR WORDS COMMUNICATE:

You aren't the center of the universe. This is the real world. If you wait until the last minute, sometimes people can't just drop everything and help you out. Especially in a family, where there are other people's time and schedules to consider.

TEEN: We have a school project we need to do. We have to get it done by Monday because that's when we present.

WHAT THEY'RE DOING:

This is classic teenager. Using school performance to tug on your heartstrings. But the bottom line is, if the project were so important, your teen should have been more prepared.

MOM: Well, I don't have time to drive you there right now.

WHAT YOUR WORDS COMMUNICATE:

I have boundaries.

TEEN: This is bull! I'm going to fail this project. You know that, right? I'm going to fail. Because of you.

MOM: Well, if you think yelling at me is going to help your case and get me to help you, you are sorely mistaken. We're done here.

TEEN: (*Yelling*) You drive her freaking everywhere and I have something I really need to do, and you won't take me!

MOM: We're not going to have this conversation if you're yelling. When you can behave like the respectful sixteen-year-old that I know you are, then we will have this conversation. Now, I have to take your sister to soccer.

> **WHAT YOUR WORDS COMMUNICATE:**
> The only way that we speak to one another in this house is calmly and with respect. If you refuse to comply with that standard, then I will simply not engage with you.

TEEN: (*Slamming the counter and throwing a towel*) God, you're the worst. Nice job parenting.

MOM: I am going to say this only one time, so it would be best if you listened. This behavior, this yelling, this tantrum is unacceptable. It has to stop now or there will be other consequences. Do you understand?

> **WHAT YOUR WORDS COMMUNICATE:**
> The only way you will ever get what you want in this house is to speak with respect to people. If you violate this rule, there will be consequences and you will lose privileges.

TEEN: (*Resigned*) Whatever.

I'm Worried My Teen Is Using Drugs

Special thanks to Dr. Robin Barnett, licensed clinical social worker, licensed clinical alcohol and drug counselor, who was consulted to address the nuances of this topic.

The Challenge

When you hear the term "drugs," your tendency might be to think that the chances of your teen getting addicted to drugs or using drugs is so statistically low that's it's basically the same as getting hit by lightning.

However, this underestimation of the prevalence and deadliness of teen drug use could be an error that could tragically hurt you and your teen.

Each year, 301,600 teenagers enter into drug and alcohol treatment programs.[12] More than 91 percent of adult drug addicts started using drugs before turning eighteen. Perhaps more alarmingly, 25 percent of people who use drugs as minors go on to become addicts, compared to only 4 percent of those who started later.[13] And drugs are particularly deadly, with roughly 120 people dying every day from drug overdose in the United States.

Your Goal

Find out if your teen is using drugs and then take the next steps to get help.

What to Expect

Teens engage in risky behavior because their brains are literally wired for it. The term "teenage brain" seems like an oxymoron to some people, but that characterization is tacitly unfair and untrue. In some ways, the teenage brain is a marvel, marked by incredible flexibility, which means that teens have the ability to take in loads of information and change dramatically with their environment. But that same plasticity is a double-edged sword. It also means that teens are more vulnerable to risky or even dangerous decisions. This is because the limbic system (which drives and controls emotions) intensifies at puberty, but the prefrontal cortex (which drives impulse control) does not fully mature until young people are in their twenties. This mismatch means teens can adapt readily to their changing environment, but also leaves them far more vulnerable to taking bad risks.

Teens use drugs for the same reasons that adults do. They take them in order to deal with the stresses and challenges of life, to overcome social anxiety, to combat isolation, and to temporarily check out from difficult feelings. These issues are intensified during the teenage years—but although this stage of life is rife with challenges, it is a temporary stage.

This all presents a good news/bad news situation. The bad news is that your teen by nature is more easily influenced, which makes him or her susceptible to taking risks with drugs. The good news is that your teen is easily influenced, which means there's likely still time for you to make a big difference if you start early. But you have to act with your eyes wide open.

Don't delude yourself. By the time most parents take action to intervene in their teenager's life to deal with the substance abuse, it is far too late and their teens are well on their way to full-fledged addiction. On the face of it, this seems tough to believe: Why would a loving parent refuse to face the clear and present fact that their teenager is using substances? And the answer is that sometimes, our love for our kids can blind us. Parents discount clear evidence because they really don't *want* to examine the idea that their teenager could be using drugs. Also, if their teenager seems to be still functioning, then they think, "If my teenager were using drugs, he or she would be curled up sweating on a mattress, unable to move for three straight days." Teenagers who use drugs often are very functional, but parents use their own experiences or misconceptions as a template, and they miss clear signs of drug use as a result.

If you discover that your teenager is experimenting with or using substances, you will likely experience a flood of difficult emotions—and you will have to fight against them. Most parents are either terrified or ashamed, two very powerful emotions that can paralyze you. If you continue to live and operate out of those emotions, you're unlikely to actually be able to help your teen. Instead of asking yourself the question "How did this happen?" you must focus all your effort and attention on the question "What can I do now to help my teen?"

Teens who are in trouble really, truly do want to get caught. Dr. Robin Barnett, a licensed clinical alcohol and drug counselor and the author of *Addict in the House: A No-Nonsense Family Guide Through Addiction and Recovery,* ran a treatment facility to help people addicted to drugs, and she said that when asked, nearly 100 percent of teens said, "I wish my parents would have known. I wish my parents would have done something." The personal and relational pain that's caused from drug addiction, the life-altering consequences that it can bring (often incredibly tragic), and the general despair that drug addiction inflicts on the lives of those ensnared by it are not something any teen truly wants. They want help as much as their parents want to give it.

What to Do

1. **Be aware of your own medicine cabinet.** It's highly likely that you (like nearly all adults) have far too much trust in your kids regarding the drugs you have in your medicine cabinet. Parents often leave their prescription drugs lying around, but you should err on the side of caution with your own medications. Many teens who use drugs often start in their parents' medicine cabinet because it's the easiest place to access drugs, there's little to no chance of getting caught, and it doesn't cost any money. For teens, it's as simple as knowing what to look for and taking it. For you, it's as simple as knowing what to look for and safely securing it.

2. **Snoop.** Teenagers by their very nature want privacy. That's the stage of life they are at. But at the end of the day, you have a legal and ethical responsibility to be aware of what is going on under your own roof. So you must snoop.* Go through their room. Look for signs of drug use. You don't have to hide this fact: Tell your teens that because they are underage and living in your house, you reserve the right to go into their room. Many of the teens who end up in rehab have fabulous, loving parents who gave their teenagers privacy because their teens didn't want them knowing what they were up to. Had those parents snooped, they could have discovered the drug abuse earlier and would have been able to spring into action to help their child before their use had developed into full-fledged addiction.

---

* I'm not suggesting you become an underground Russian operative and wiretap your teen's phone. Unless you *are* a Russian operative. In which case, please proceed.

3. **OVERREACT, because your tendency will be to underreact.** Imagine that it was brought to your attention that your teenager was stealing something from friends at school—you would likely have a very strong reaction. You would talk to the other parents, you would talk to your teen, and you'd make a big deal of it because you would want to teach your teen that stealing is wrong. That it hurts people. That it hurts them. You'd need to make a point. So if your kid comes home drunk, you have to make a big deal out of it, and this will be a tipping point. Immediately take concrete actions: Rearrange your calendar to prioritize the issue, get a professional involved, and adopt a serious tone and attitude. If you do this, your teen will either work incredibly hard to hide his or her substance abuse (and if you're paying attention, you'll likely see those cues, which will confirm your suspicion that your teen does indeed have a problem) or your teen will say, "Dear heaven. This is way too much of a hassle. I'm not going to do that anymore."

4. **Don't be afraid to drug-test your teen.** If you suspect that your teenager is using drugs, make them take a drug test. You can buy over-the-counter drug tests at any drugstore. These tests show results for many of the most commonly abused substances. This way you will have conclusive proof, either negative or positive. Your teens will fight you on this, and it's likely that they will get offended and upset. It's also likely to put a very real emotional strain on you. But you simply must have hard evidence. It will either prove their innocence or give you actionable information you can use to truly help them. Remember your motives: Your goal is to love and help your teen. When in their right mind, nearly all teens instinctively know when an adult is acting in their best interests, even if they resist and fight along the way.

5. **Get professional help. Seriously.** Many parents, once they discover that their teen is using drugs, try to handle the situation themselves, letting fear and shame rule their reaction. Often, with good intentions, they think something like "I'm a good parent. I can take care of this." But you can't. Once someone has started using drugs, two things happen: They morph into a liar and they morph into a thief.

You are dealing with an entirely different teen. Getting professional help takes the game of "who is telling the truth?" out of it, and it shows your teen that you are serious and mean business. You must make this a very, very big issue. The best-case scenario: Your teen was only experimenting and the whole process of counseling scares them straight. The worst-case scenario: Your teen was deeper into addiction than you knew and now they get the professional help they need for a chance to beat addiction.

How Does a Normal, Everyday Teen Become a Drug Addict?

Dr. Robin Barnett ran a drug treatment facility in New Jersey for years that treated tens of thousands of teens. We asked her if there was a common narrative among teens admitted into her facility. Barnett said she saw one particular story line play out not dozens of times, not hundreds of times, but thousands of times. Are there other paths that teens take to get involved in illegal drug use? Of course. But this is by far the clearest and most likely path that teens take toward addiction.

Step 1: Your teen is bored.

They aren't involved in any extracurricular activities that feed their natural desire for fun, belonging, and freedom. This provides a gap in fulfillment and meaning in a young person's life.

Step 2: Your teen goes into your medicine cabinet.

When polled, most parents believe that the most likely place for their teen to encounter illegal drugs for the first time is when it's introduced to them by a friend at a party. Experts say differently: The vast majority of kids who start using drugs start in their parents' medicine cabinet, usually with pain pills prescribed to the parents by a doctor. This is the easiest place to access drugs. Teens know they have little to no chance of getting caught, it doesn't cost them money, and it's as simple as knowing what kind of pills to look for and then taking them.

Step 3: The pills work.

Teens don't start using hard drugs. Pills seem unthreatening. And they make your teen feel good. The pain pills medicate some underlying issue such as anxiety, stress, or depression, and if a teen encounters something that immediately relieves those symptoms, that's gold.

Step 4: Your teen finishes the bottle.

By now, your teen is actively searching out the experience provided to them by the pills, but the supply is not endless.

Step 5: Your teen attempts to purchase more pills.

The stats all say that your teen's supplier is likely to be someone they know from school. The problem is, these prescription pills are expensive (for example, OxyContin sells for roughly $30 to $40 per pill), so the teen begins to figure out a way to steal money from his or her parents. But that supply of money is also usually finite.

Step 6: Your teen finds a cheaper solution to opiate pills.

Knowing that opiate pills such as OxyContin have become too expensive on the street, drug cartels in Mexico did two things: They dramatically increased production of the drug heroin (which is much easier and cheaper to make), and they developed networks to move it across the nation. As of 2015, the cost of a pack of cigarettes in New York City was $10.29. In 2015, a bindle (a bag containing a single hit) of heroin went for about $10 a bag.[14]

Step 7: Your teen begins experimenting with heroin by snorting it.

Someone will tell your teen that heroin is far more addictive when injected directly into the bloodstream, and that it is far less so when snorted (in powder form) or smoked. This is fundamentally untrue, but it sounds true to your teen. So your teen either snorts a line or smokes a joint with heroin in it. The drug enters the bloodstream through the nasal and sinus passages, creating an almost instantaneous high. From the first hit, your teen is now physically addicted to the drug.

Step 8: Your teen's tolerance builds.

Heroin blocks sensations of pain and causes sedation or euphoria when it binds to opioid receptor cells in the brain. In its molecular structure, heroin is closely related to morphine, and when your teen smokes or snorts heroin, their body converts the drug quickly to morphine. Morphine provides the rush of pleasure and profound relaxation. But heroin is classified by the Drug Enforcement Administration as a Schedule I substance, defined as drugs with no currently accepted medical use and a high potential for abuse. It doesn't take long for your teen's brain to adjust to the impact of heroin. The brain gets used to an elevated level of opioids. At this point, your teen simply needs more heroin to achieve the same high.

Step 9: Someone introduces your teen to a needle.

Over time, as your teen needs more and more heroin to achieve the same high, someone will introduce him or her to the concept of injecting heroin directly into the bloodstream. By now your teen is physically addicted to one of the most dangerous and addictive drugs on the planet. Your teen's brain, which constantly seeks a state of balance, tries to restore the former level of opioids by triggering intense cravings for heroin. Because of the severity of these cravings and the intense discomfort of withdrawal, heroin is notoriously hard to quit. Your teen simply cannot overcome these cravings and is now a full-fledged addict.

Just so we're clear: The point of outlining the path to drug addiction was not to frighten you or to imply that the above scenario is somehow inevitable. It's not. There is strong evidence—validated by research— that parents and caring adults can alter, interrupt, and even reverse this path. The National Institute on Drug Abuse[15] found that one of the strongest protective factors preventing teen drug abuse is parental support, and also found that factors like parental monitoring and supervision are critical for drug abuse prevention in teens. As a parent, you matter more than you realize and have more influence than it sometimes feels. Don't doubt your influence; lean into it.

THE STATE OF THE TEENAGE UNION: DRUG USE

The following statistics about teen behavior were reported by the US Centers for Disease Control and Prevention's Youth Risk Behavior Surveillance System. These sobering numbers show the true prevalence of drug use among teens, and should serve as a wake-up call for all of us.[16]

63.2 percent of high school students have had alcohol

38.6 percent have used marijuana

32.8 percent currently drink alcohol

21.7 percent were offered, sold, or given an illegal drug on school property

21.7 percent currently use marijuana

17.7 percent drink five or more drinks of alcohol in a row

17.2 percent drank alcohol for the first time before age thirteen

16.8 percent took prescription drugs without a doctor's prescription

7.5 percent tried marijuana for the first time before age thirteen

7.0 percent have used inhalants

6.4 percent have used hallucinogenic drugs

5.0 percent have used cocaine and Ecstasy

4.3 percent have had ten or more drinks in a row

3.0 percent have used methamphetamines

2.1 percent have used heroin

1.8 percent have injected any illegal drug

I'm Worried My Teen Is Sexting

Special thanks to Dr. Hal Pickett, child and adolescent psychologist at Headway Emotional Health Services, who was consulted to address the nuances of this topic.

The Challenge

Kellie thinks Zack is cute. Zack asks for her cell phone number. They start talking. They start Snapchatting. They start going out. Zack asks Kellie to take a provocative picture for him. She takes one. He asks to see more. She stands in front of her bathroom mirror and takes a full-length picture of herself naked. She sends it to him. Zack sees it. Zack screenshots it. Kellie thinks he deleted it, but Zack saved the photo to his phone. A few weeks later, Zack and Kellie break up. Zack forwards the nude photo to his friend, a girl who used to be friends with Kellie. She superimposes some text on the picture. "Ho Alert!" she types. "If you think this girl is a whore, then text this to all your friends." Then she clicks open the long list of contacts on her phone and presses send.

In less than twenty-four hours, it's as though Kellie had sauntered naked down the hallways of four high schools. Hundreds, perhaps thousands, of students have now seen the photo.

And Kellie's life is changed forever.

This happens hundreds of times per year to students all across the world. And even if the scenario is not as hair-raising and public as the story of Zack and Kellie, there are regular news stories covering related incidents.

Sexting, defined, is sending someone sexually explicit photographs or messages via a mobile phone. Up to 20 percent of teens are found to engage in sexting, and while studies vary widely, roughly 10 percent have sent a sexually explicit image, and as many as 20 percent have received such an image.[17]

In recent years, with the ubiquity of the Internet, teens are being inundated more and more with provocative images. And yet all the numbers and all the research shows that sexting can go really wrong and affect a teen's life in dramatic ways. Here's what you need to know to help your teen avoid these devastating outcomes.

Your Goal

To prevent the devastating situation where naked pictures of your teenager are circulated online.

What to Expect

Your teen likely doesn't know sexting is illegal. Maybe you don't either. But depending on the state involved, sexting has very real legal ramifications. In many states, if a teenager sends naked pictures of a person under the age of eighteen (even if they send pictures of themselves), that is prosecutable under the charge of trafficking in child pornography. Additionally, different states have different legal ages for the "age of consent," which means the legal age when teenagers can make choices (legally) about their own sexual activity. So, for example, in the state of Minnesota, the age of consent is sixteen, so if someone is seventeen and is dating someone fifteen or younger, then the exchange of sexually explicit photos could carry with it other legal ramifications, such as corruption of a minor or other statutory codes. In theory, this could result in charging the older party as a sex offender, and requiring him or her to register as a sex offender.

The point is this: Although most teens understand that sexting isn't smart, they don't have any idea that it's illegal.

The sexting issue is complex and emotionally tricky. Sometimes teens don't even see a problem with sexting, and may be excited about doing it because it's sexually arousing or affirming. But sometimes things take a turn for the worse. And when it comes to sexting gone wrong, it's usually girls who feel the pain.

To start, girls are more likely to deal with unwanted sexting. They are also more likely to face peer pressure by a boy or their boyfriend to sext ("just send me a picture") and even by more provocative girls as well ("send him a nude pic—it's the only way you'll ever get a boyfriend"). And to cap things off, they are typically the ones who are harmed in situations of sexting gone wrong. This is a generalization (and of course there are boys who have to deal with this), but there seems to be a firm double standard in our society when it comes to sexting—and girls are the ones most often shamed.

When a picture that was supposed to be private is shared, whether it's to dozens of people or even to just a few friends beyond the intended recipient, many girls feel sexually violated. In fact, psychologists and counselors say that the psychological trauma caused by sexting-related incidents has many of the same symptoms as actual physical assault: deep feelings of mistrust, profound insecurity, depression, self-blaming, shame, and humiliation.

If you discover that your teen has been sexting, you're going to need to stay calm. Understandably, most parents have a very strong emotional reaction when they find out their teenager has been sending and/or receiving sexually explicit photos and messages with another teen. This can be for a variety of reasons. You could flare up because you want to protect them: You know how dangerous sexting can be in our digital age, and they likely don't. Another reason is that you have to come face-to-face with the harsh reality that your little boy or little girl is a sexual being. But regardless of the reason, the point is this: When you're dealing with the rawness of emotions that stem from your own issues, don't process those in front of your children. Crying or yelling or screaming or ranting won't help anyone. Including you.

What to Do

1. **Help your teen see that sexting leads to the wrong type of popularity**, and that although it might bring attention to his or her body, what's most important about people is not their physical body. It's their heart, their mind, their feelings, their dreams, their aspirations. That's the real you, the most important part of you. Explain that if someone is interested only in getting to know his or her body and doesn't care at all about the other things that make them them, then that person is not worth their time. As the meme says, "If your boyfriend wants you for your breasts, legs, and thighs, send him to KFC. You're a person, not a cheap value meal."

2. **Say something clear and blunt like this: "Do not take pictures of your naked body and send them to someone else."** When it comes to teenagers, there is an absolute lack of information and education about sexting. So before you even give your teens a cell phone, have this conversation with them and explain why it's so important.

3. **If consensual sexting has occurred, read the situation.** The most important thing that needs to happen is that the two teenagers involved need to talk to an adult whom they trust in order to discuss the ramifications of sexting. If done the right way, this can yield dividends and really help teens. If you know the other teen (and especially if you know the other teen's parents), a good strategy might be to contact them in hopes of having a sit-down with all parties involved. Don't do this if you have reason to believe that the other teenager's parents (or parent) aren't reasonable or engaged. And make sure you give the other family time to sit with the information and process it. Like you, the other adults need time to get out of panic and shock mode so they

can have a reasonable conversation. So begin by reading the situation, but be sure an adult talks openly with both teens.

4. **If consensual sexting has occurred, but something bad has happened, be ready to listen empathically.** Most of the time, parents and adults come in, lectures ready and loaded. But that doesn't work well. You need to create an environment in which your teen will be willing to share. Here are some questions you might ask:

- How are you feeling about this?
- Do you know the laws around this stuff?
- Did you feel pressured to do this?
- What do you need from me? What would you like me to do?

5. **If sexting has occurred and pictures of your teen are widely circulated, get professional help.** Again, this is the worst-case scenario, and all of the other steps should be taken to prevent and avoid this scenario. But if this has happened, you must get your teen to see a professional counselor who can help deal with the fallout.

I'm Worried My Teen Is Cutting

Special thanks to Dr. Fran Walfish, a family and relationship psychotherapist and expert contributor to this chapter.

The Challenge

In Mindset #1: Teens Need You More Than It Seems, we talked about Holden Caulfield, the unreliable narrator and protagonist in J.D. Salinger's book *The Catcher in the Rye*. Over the years, Holden has become an icon for teenage rebellion and angst. But he is also tragically misunderstood.

Because although in many ways, Holden is a walking ball of contradictions just like any other teenager, he is markedly different in one key area. Holden is carrying within himself a depth of pain that few teens can understand, because his beloved younger brother, Allie, passed away from leukemia. In one of the most tender and revealing parts of the book, he recounts the night Allie died.

That night Holden slept in his family's garage. With his parents emotionally unavailable to him, he is unable to process the weight of his own tremendous grief. So he breaks every window in the garage with his fist, like a wounded animal flying into a rage. The only thing preventing him from breaking the windows on the family station wagon is the fact that his hand is already cut, bleeding, and badly broken. In recalling this event, Holden admits that it was stupid, but then immediately gets defensive, saying, "You didn't know Allie."

The damage to Holden's hand because of this violent outburst is lasting: He reveals that even at this point he can't make a fist and that his hand sometimes aches when it rains. Holden dismisses the permanent impact of this injury, saying that he was never planning on being a surgeon or a violinist, anyway, but the point has already been made. Holden's heart wasn't the only thing that broke the night Allie died.

This episode is just textbook Holden. But it's also textbook teenagers. Teens, when faced with incredible emotional stress, if they have no trusted adults to turn to, will often manifest a maladaptive coping method called self-injury.

Nonsuicidal self-injury, often simply called self-injury, is the act of deliberately harming the surface of your own body, such as cutting or burning yourself. Recent community studies have found that a third to a half of US teenagers have engaged in some type of nonsuicidal self-injury.[18]

But here's the problem: Although distinct from suicidal behavior, cutting (and other forms of self-harm) frequently occurs in adolescents who at other times have contemplated or attempted suicide. Parents and adults need to take cutting seriously and understand its dangers—not just physiologically, but psychologically.

What to Expect

Teens who cut frequently do so by using a razor blade to make small cuts—almost always parallel to the wrist—on the area of the arm between the wrist and the elbow. The cuts are usually not vertical (that type of cut is far more dangerous to make and can be a sign of a suicidal attempt). As such, teens who cut typically attempt to mask or hide these cuts, so they will wear long sleeves, even in situations where such clothing makes little practical sense.

The implications for your teen are uncomfortable to examine. Many teens report that cutting helps them feel more alive.[19] But cutting and self-harm are considered "maladaptive," meaning they are inadequate, unhelpful, or unhealthy coping mechanisms. As you can imagine, cutting doesn't help your teen long-term. It's a big red flag and parents *must* pay serious attention to it. This is compounded for parents because if you talk to teens who are cutting, they will often tell you that you are overreacting. But according to research,[20] cutting, once thought to be a coping mechanism for some individuals in distress, may also open the door to more dangerous actions by lowering one's inhibitions to suicidal thoughts and behaviors. Parents should seek immediate help.

The implications for you are also uncomfortable to examine. This is unpleasant to write, but in talking with numerous counselors and psychologists, this is the harsh truth: Any child or teen who is cutting is dealing with emotional pain and feels there is no warm, open, safe place within the family to go and talk about it. Teens cut because they feel utterly alone, abandoned, or ignored by the adults in their lives.

What to Do

1. **Fight past shame, guilt, and denial and keep your priorities straight.** Many parents, when they discover that their teen is engaging in self-harm, are confronted with some very difficult ideas. First is the general pain that your teenager could be suicidal. Many parents can't bear the pain of facing that idea, so they minimize it. It's critical that you don't do this. Second, many parents begin to ask, "Where did I fail?" and think because their teen is in trouble that it reflects poorly on them. Don't resist getting help because you're afraid of what strangers might think. And you need to be kind to yourself, too. All of us have limitations. You can give only what you've got and what you've been given, and you've done your best with that. Keep your priorities straight: Get help for your teen and for yourself. Through this process, it truly is possible that both you and your teen will heal.

2. **Secure the house.** If you discover that your teen is cutting, the first order of business is to keep your teen safe by removing any dangerous objects. Go through the house and safely secure all blades, cutting devices, razors, knives, or other sharp objects.

3. **Get qualified help.** Never criticize. Never judge. Never blame. Never point fingers. Never make bargains. Just get help. Parents should reach out for professional help right away. You cannot handle this on your own, and that's okay. In dealing with a teenager who is engaging in cutting (or other forms of self-harm), you are no longer within the norm of what regular, everyday parents can handle. You need a specialist. See "How to Convince Your Teen to Get Help" (page 147), which explains how to choose an ideal counselor and how to convince your teen to engage in counseling.

The benefits of seeing professional counselors are innumerable. First off, your struggling teen will have a dedicated professional to listen to them. This in and of itself is tremendously healing. Second, oftentimes teens participate in group therapy, and this group experience is very powerful. When teens are in a group setting with other teens who are their age and who feel exactly the same way, there is a real power that comes from seeing themselves in others and knowing they're not alone.

Additionally, with counseling, teens emerge with a set of useful tactics. They are trained and given a practical list of strategies they can turn to when they feel overwhelmed or triggered. These include ways to deal with intense emotions (draw, paint, journal), self-soothe (take a bath, listen to calming music), fight off feelings of being disconnected (call a therapist or friend), release tension (exercise rigorously, rip paper, use a stress ball), and stop feeling numb (chew on something with a very strong taste, like cinnamon gum or a grapefruit peel). When your teen has been hopeless and lifeless, seeing him or her change into a young person full of life is worth an awful lot.

I'm Worried My Teen Is Stressed Out

Special thanks to Dr. Jennifer Freed, executive director of the AHA! teen program, who was consulted to address the nuances of this topic.

The Challenge

Psychologist Lawrence J. Cohen, in his *Time* article "The Drama of the Anxious Child," recalls learning when he was studying psychology in the early eighties that in any population of children, about 10 to 20 percent will be kids who by nature are uneasy and nervous about anything new or unfamiliar. Some of these children grow into teens who are naturally more anxious or shy about new situations, but in the eighties, only a small percentage (around 1 to 5 percent) would go on to develop and receive a diagnosis for anxiety disorder.

Today there's still likely the same percentage of kids who are naturally shy and cautious (10 to 20 percent), but according to the National Institute for Mental Health, the number of young people who go on to be diagnosed with anxiety disorders has skyrocketed to 25 percent.[21]

Across the nation, educators are seeing more and more students suffering from depression, anxiety, and social phobia. The acuity of mental illness among students has sharpened, they say, and it's striking ever younger children. Many quietly bear the stress for years before breaking.

And a study published by the journal *Psychiatric Clinics of North America* confirms that "there is persuasive evidence from a range of studies that anxiety disorders are the most frequent mental disorders in children and adolescents."[22]

What the heck is going on? Why are kids more stressed, less able to cope with that stress, and dealing with low-grade anxiety all the time? And how can we, as caring adults, help?

The good news is that there are some pretty simple steps that you can take with your teen that will dramatically decrease the amount of anxiety and stress that they feel.

Your Goal

To help your teen deal with stress and anxiety in a healthy way.

What to Expect

Understand what low-grade anxiety and stress look like in a teenager. Here are some common signs:

- Restlessness or feeling wound-up or on edge
- Being easily fatigued
- Difficulty concentrating or having their minds go blank
- Irritability
- Muscle tension
- Difficulty controlling their worry
- Sleep problems (difficulty falling or staying asleep, or restless, unsatisfying sleep)

Every teen deals with anxiety at some level.* The simple rites of passage for adolescents are tough enough to navigate and add anxiety by default. But the modern world adds stress to teenagers' lives in ways that you might not fully understand:

- College admission is significantly more competitive, and as a result, high school is more competitive and stressful.
- Teenagers are overscheduled. Between homework, AP classes, sports practices, extracurriculars like music and student government, SAT prep, girlfriends and boyfriends, jobs, and friends, kids don't have much free time these days.
- As a result of not having enough time to do "nothing" and enjoy the downtime needed to process all their new experiences, teens often feel overwhelmed.
- The modern economy puts a lot of financial pressure on families, adding stress that trickles down to teens.
- Near-constant entertainment choices send teens on a quest to "never be bored," which is an impossible demand.
- Part of being a teenager means making connections outside of the family. But social media creates environments filled with either instant gratification of a teenager's sense of self or opportunities for criticism, bullying, and disapproval. This is difficult to navigate.
- Digital screens, the coping mechanism of choice, are not actually effective ways of coping. At a time when teens are more digitally connected than ever, they are also more isolated, anxious, and depressed.

---

* I mean, think about it. At the very moment you want to be the most charming, elegant, and cool for your crush—it is the *exact* moment Mother Nature unleashes the destructive power of puberty.

What to Do

1. **The most persistent and reliable mechanism for reducing anxiety is spending time with your teen that is not interrupted in any way by screens.** The removal of the distraction of screens enables meaningful conversation. This will allow teens to begin to process their emotions and dramatically increases the chance they're going to open up to you about what's going on in their hearts and minds. Paying attention to your teen helps him or her feel valued and listened to. Talking helps your teen process the complexity of life. This is soothing and reduces anxiety. And sharing out loud helps your teen feel connected to someone. Finally, uninterrupted time together models for teens the most healthy and successful strategy for anxiety reduction and happiness: human connection.

2. **Encourage your teen to unplug.** According to a Kaiser Family Foundation media study, teens spend more than nine hours a day consuming media.[23] Nine hours.[24] This hyperconnectivity—constant notifications, refreshing, wondering "did they like my post?!"—is a part of the problem when it comes to stress. Push teens to intentionally detach from their screens. Not forever. ("Mom, what's next, churning our own butter?") But for a period of time. Because it's what they need. And if we're being honest, this isn't just a teen thing, is it? So be sure to lead by example.

3. **Do something together.** After your teen (and you!) unplug, get out and do something with your newfound abundance of time. We interviewed parents for some activities that they found worked well. Here are the best ideas we encountered:

- Go on a walk in nature with your teen. The slowness and the simple beauty of nature will begin to shift his or her brain.
- Go on a camping trip. You and your teen have to collaborate to figure out where to go and then plan what you need to bring

and work together to get it ready. Such a project is also, by definition, very task-oriented and physical (setting up the tent, making the fire, etc.).

- Cook together and prepare a special meal together. So many teens don't have the foggiest idea how to cook, and this is a practical real-world skill. Cooking also engages all the senses, and by its very nature it is a collaborative activity that makes people feel connected.

- If your teen is kinesthetic and you are handy, do a project in the house together (paint a room, build patio furniture, etc.).

- If you and your teen have an artistic bent, create art together. Take a painting or photography class together (something interesting to both of you that you're sharing side by side).

- Do something athletic together, like riding bikes or learning how to surf. Sign up for a philanthropic race and train for it together.

- Find a way to do community service together. There's also a hidden, long-term benefit as teens learn to seek meaning in activities instead of simply pleasure. We all feel better when we do something that helps another human being.

If you implement these actions, here's what will happen. It involves a psychological term called co-regulation, which means that the parent and the child help each other feel better. The most easy-to-see example of this is a mother with her newborn. The mother, sensitive to the baby, speaks in tender, sweet language. And the baby hears these words and coos and giggles, which causes the mother to smile and kiss the baby, which causes the baby to smile back. Both, mysteriously and dynamically, are helping each other. This is the miracle of human connection. And yes, it's true your teen isn't a baby anymore. But teens still do need reassurance, someone to listen to them, and someone to encourage them.

TEENS AND TECH HEADACHES

FADE IN: *EXT.—LATE AFTERNOON An apartment complex*
DISSOLVE TO: *INT., FAMILY ROOM*
Seated on the couch, looking up are MONICA, a fifteen-year-old whose dark hair is pulled back, and LEEBO, her thirteen-year-old brother, who is wearing a sports jersey that looks almost awkwardly big on him. Standing over them is MOM, who is pacing.

LEEBO: Okay, who called this meeting?

MOM: I did.

LEEBO: That was a joke, Mom.

MOM: We need to make some changes. As your mother, I just feel that this is on me.

MONICA: What kind of changes?

MOM: It's about this. (*She pulls out her cell phone and shakes it*) This.

LEEBO: Okay. You don't like Samsung. Get an iPhone.

MOM: No, that's just it. I don't want a new phone. I want no phone.

MONICA: You don't want a cell phone?

MOM: I don't want any of this. This. (*Points to her cell phone*) This is taking over our lives. No! It's *ruining* our lives.

MONICA: I mean, it's not ruining . . .

MOM: Yes. Have you read the studies? Because I have. I will not let these devices come into *my* home and turn *my* children into brain-dead, emotionally stunted zombies incapable of actually interacting with actual humans. I don't want you to have the attention span of a gnat.

MONICA: I'm sorry. What were you saying?

MOM: It's not funny!

LEEBO: No, you're right. It's not funny when your mom loses her mind.

MOM: Or have I gained my mind? Hmmm?

LEEBO: (*Looking at his sister*) No. You've lost it.

MOM: So starting today, no more cell phones. No Internet. No cable. Nothing in our home.

MONICA: Whoa, what?

MOM: We're cutting all cords. We're going off the grid!

LEEBO: Mom I feel like you're about thirty seconds from telling us that we're going to churn our own butter.

MOM: Great idea. But don't get smart with me.

MONICA: How will we settle debates about obscure facts?

MOM: Like what?

MONICA: Like, if Twinkies are actually cake.

LEEBO: They're not.

MOM: (*Surprised*) They're not?

LEEBO: Nope. They never see an oven. They're complex lipids injected with chemical catalysts.

MOM: And that's why we need to get off the grid. Because that's not natural.

MONICA: Mom. How am I supposed to do my homework?

MOM: The old-fashioned way. With a pencil, a piece of paper, and an abacus.

LEEBO: What's an abacus?

MONICA: I think it's an app.

MOM: This will change our lives for the better.

LEEBO: Mom. How am I supposed to talk to my friends?

MOM: Visit them. Ride your bike to their house, like we did back when I was growing up.

LEEBO: You mean like a pedal bike? With pedals? Can I just Uber? (*To himself*) No, I can't call an Uber. I won't have a phone.

MOM: This is going to save your brain.

MONICA: Mom, this isn't practical. Technology is part of life.

MOM: It's not natural.

LEEBO: Plastics aren't natural, either. You're not going to stop using plastics.

MOM: Plastics don't rot your brain and destroy human relationships.

MONICA: I think somebody's brain has been rotted.

MOM: I heard that.

MONICA: That was the point.

LEEBO: Mom! I want to major in computer science. That's going to require that I use a computer.

MOM: Enough back talk. This is what we're doing.

MONICA: I get it, Mom. You're freaked out about technology. It's okay. We can set guidelines. This . . . this just seems extreme.

MOM: Desperate times call for desperate measures. I will not lose my children to technology.

LEEBO: No. You're going to lose your children the old-fashioned way. By going crazy.

MOM: Technology will not destroy my family. I won't let it.

MONICA: That's fine, Mom. I just think there's a middle ground.

MOM: No. Machines are the enemy. Technology is the enemy.

LEEBO: Listen, Sarah Connor. Skynet isn't active yet.

MOM: Machines are the enemy!

NARRATOR: Like many parents, this mom is afraid of what the changing tech world will mean for her kids. Here's how you can help your teens utilize technology without being controlled by it, and also help them be a responsible digital citizen.

Healthy Boundaries Around Screen Time

Special thanks to Dr. Gene Beresin, professor of psychiatry at Harvard Medical School and executive director of the Clay Center for Young Healthy Minds at Massachusetts General Hospital, who was consulted to address the nuances of this topic.

The Challenge

In 1920, when the radio first became a mass-consumer product, it was viewed by some as the herald of a new age of communication and by others as "the devil's work." Many thought listening to music or drama at home instead of in theaters and parks would completely dismantle the communal experience of music.

But by 1950, teenagers began using the radio to listen to music they liked, and through that shared experience, a whole genre of music was birthed. Teenagers used the radio to connect to one another in ways that adults thought was sure to destroy the modern world.

In 1948, there were thirty million phones in the United States. By 1960, there were eighty million. And again, adults became concerned as teenagers would leave school, go to one another's houses, and then return home in the evening and spend hours talking to one another on their landline phones

Cut to the present day, when according to the Pew Research Center, 88 percent of twelve- to seventeen-year-olds have a cell phone and 92 percent of teens go online daily.[25]

Fact #1: Teens will always use the newest technologies to connect with one another.

Fact #2: Parents will always be concerned about the effects of the newest technologies on their teens.

Teens love technology because it allows them to flock to places (both physical and digital) where other teenagers are and adults are not. Part of this is because the psychological drive of a teenager is toward autonomy and identity. Adolescence is a time of figuring out how they are different from their parents and how they are the same—and connections to other teens helps them do that.

Today, a full 90 percent of teenagers are online. Roughly 63 percent of teenagers exchange text messages daily (that number will likely continue to climb), 50 percent of teenagers log onto social media at least once per day, and 22 percent of teenagers log onto social media more than ten times a day. And adults, like their parents and their parents before them, are worried about the effect that technology is having on the development of their children.

But in our modern world, how can parents and caring adults help teenagers navigate through this digital era? How much interaction with technology is too much? When can technology begin hurting a teenager?

Your Goal

To help your teen become a well-rounded person who can coexist with technology and not be ruled by it.

What to Expect

Pushback: Nearly 88 percent of teens are online and have cell phones. Their cell phone is not a tech device, it's a relational device. And teens primarily use technology to connect with their friends and peers.

(Teens also use technology to consume a never-ending stream of cat memes. As do I. No judgment here.)

So when you begin to talk about restrictions on that device, it's going to feel to teens like an assault on their friendships and their ability to know what's going on in their world. This feeling is fair. I mean, don't you get twitchy when you've got to set your phone to airplane mode for a few hours? Knowing this, be understanding when it comes to talking about screen-time boundaries. Explain that you realize how important it is to be able to talk to and connect with their friends, but that having a cell phone is a privilege, not a right. If you acknowledge their needs and honestly discuss your concerns, you'll get a lot further. And remember, you have leverage here. Teens desperately want their phones. So use that to your advantage to set up some fair and clear agreed-upon rules. I'll show you how to do so later in this section.

All parents want to know the exact number of minutes per day that their teens should (or should not) be interacting with technology. Adults are afraid there's a magic threshold, and if their teens ingest more media than that, they'll turn into mindless robots. But there are simply too many variables to assign a one-time-fits-all mandate—there is no magic number. It's like asking, "How much money should I withdraw from my bank account?" For one person, withdrawing $100 would be perfectly fine. For another, it would be an overdraft. The point is, each teenager's unique learning and attention issues, processing speed, and ability to accomplish other important goals in life create a far more nuanced matrix than a simple time limit. This boundary requires careful parental observation and should be based more on intuition and the overall health of your particular teen than on a magic number.

What to Do

1. **Know your teen.** The first question that parents always ask is: How many minutes per day should my teenager be allowed to be on

a screen? And this is a great question, but a better question is: How is my teenager fulfilling his or her most important priorities? These include:

- Doing well academically
- Participating in the family
- Spending time face-to-face with their friends
- Spending time engaging in other interests
- Getting enough exercise
- Getting enough sleep

If your teen is socially isolated, spending large amounts of time in his or her room alone on the phone and not interacting with friends or family, that's a red flag. If your teen is missing dinner or family activities to play video games, that's a red flag. If your teen is up all night or is so drowsy in the morning he or she can't get up, that's a red flag. And if your teen's grades are slipping, those are all reasons to seriously evaluate and have conversations about the health of your teen's interaction with media and technology.

Screen time becomes problematic when it interferes with areas that are important for developing maturity in teens. Try asking this question: "How is my teenager performing in key areas that really matter in the development of his or her social maturity?" If you have a kid who is doing all of the things on the list above, then you have to ask yourself, "Why am I worried about this?" And the answer to that is "Maybe you shouldn't be." But if you have any intuitions or misgivings about your teen and his or her overall well-being, then maybe it's time to have some hard conversations with yourself and with your teen.

2. **Cut them off at night.** Teenagers are naturally programmed to stay up late. Every human has a group of nerve cells in the brain called the suprachiasmatic nucleus, which operates like a "master clock" telling the body when it's time to be alert and when it's time to wind down. Oddly enough, even though teenagers need more sleep at this stage of their life than at any other time (besides infancy), their body clocks

and circadian rhythms run later than at any other point in their lives. Teenage minds process information at night and consolidate the day's learning at night. So there's a reason your teen is a night owl, and it's biological.

That's the good news. The bad news is that the ultraviolet light from screens (any screen) gets processed by the optic nerves and sends messages to the brain that it's not time to wind down, even though it's ten at night and dark outside. This can disrupt your teenager's sleep.

Don't prolong your teen's day by allowing him or her to interact with screens at night. A good idea is to have a charging station somewhere in the home, where teens can put their phones, iPads, and other flat-screen devices at some point midevening. This will not only remove the strong temptation for teens to be on their screens at night (texting their friends, YouTube marathons, and whatnot), but it will also help their circadian rhythms calm down.

I've tried to lead by example in my own home by intentionally limiting the hours I'm on devices and by communicating that to my family so they keep me in check.

3. **Use media to slingshot into meaningful conversation.** If you've established good ground rules and boundaries around media consumption, then use media to dive into the heart and mind of your teen. Talk about what they're watching. If you are flexible and nimble, you can catch your teenager and steal some great conversations. There are three main times when you can usually sneak in a conversation about what they're watching and seeing on media: driving time, dinnertime, and evenings. Ask your teen questions like:

- I know you loved that movie. What made you like it so much?
- That character—some people don't think he's heroic. What do you think?
- It's interesting we both love this show. Why do you think we like it so much?
- There's a lot of buzz around [insert celebrity] saying/doing that thing. What are your thoughts on it?

- Did you see that [insert recent news or political event]? There's been a lot of outrage about it. Do you think people are over-reacting, or do they have a point?

Ask your kids what bands they're watching and listening to, and ask to see one of that band's videos. Ask your teenagers for their opinions about current events that they're seeing on the news. And you can even have metaconversations about media itself. Ask your teen:

- What do you see in my life in terms of my media habits?
- Do you notice anything I do that's healthy or unhealthy?

And then listen. The fact that your teen is invited to speak about your life is tremendously encouraging to him or her. Teens need help from parents to develop good skills for media hygiene and social connection. Having conversations is a great way to help them—and to make meaningful connections at the same time.

Helping Them Think About What They Post Online

The Challenge

At some point, your teen will move from being simply a consumer who uses the Internet to watch cat videos and listen to music to being a creator of online content. The emerging generation has a voracious appetite for participating in and contributing to social networks. Fully 55 percent have posted a selfie on a social media site, and according to the Pew Research Center, 27 percent of Internet-using teens ages twelve through seventeen have recorded and uploaded a video to the Internet.

The Internet has proven to be a powerful form of social connection, and it has allowed for self-expression at an incredible rate. But things can easily take a wrong turn.

A few years ago, a teenage Burger King employee from Cleveland took a picture of himself with his feet in the bins of lettuce they use for burgers. He posted it online anonymously. Safe, right? Wrong. Burger King found out and traced the photo back to his phone. Not only was he fired, but Burger King corporate fired the entire crew he worked with. Every single one of them. Hey, buddy. Have it your way.

It's not all momentary idiocy that downgrades your future job prospects in a burger kingdom, though. The advent of social media has also seen teenagers compete in various online challenges. Some of these can be dangerous, like the "salt and ice challenge" that had teens videoing themselves competing to see who could withstand the pain of rubbing salt and ice on their skin the longest. In the process, some gave themselves second-degree burns and in several severe cases even required skin grafts, according to doctors at Riley Hospital for Children at Indiana University.

These types of scenarios are something teenagers today have to deal with—something that, frankly, you and I never had to even think about. As one parent I was talking to recently said, "The best part of being in my thirties is that I did all my stupid stuff before the Internet."

That comment might make you chuckle, but in the modern world, your teen's digital footprint is no laughing matter. What they post, write, and upload can either help or hurt them. And it's up to you to empower your teen to make good decisions with this new wave of technology—and to help them understand that social media, like all privileges, is a responsibility.

The Goal

The goal is to coach teens to think about what they are creating and posting online and the implications of that content on their future.

What to Expect

For teens, the Internet is inherently social—it isn't merely a place for entertainment or learning, but a place where their friends are. But as in all other areas of their social life, teens are trying things out socially. And there are so many built-in social reward mechanisms on the Internet to encourage your teenager to generate content—to take pictures of themselves, post comments and likes to friends, etc. But because their brains are developing (and because they have not had as much life experience), teens often push the boundaries of what it means to be social. They learn by doing things they shouldn't and making mistakes. The problem is, the Internet can archive all of those mistakes.

Your teen isn't thinking about this. There are certain things that just aren't on your teen's radar—say, property taxes or the potential implications of the consumer price index on the global economy–and this includes the dangers of the Internet. And because the social power of the Internet is so overwhelming, most teens are only vaguely aware of the potential issues. For example, they're not thinking about the implications of posting that photo that clearly shows their home address. And they certainly aren't thinking about making their online presence look appealing to colleges and future employers. They're too preoccupied with getting likes, shares, and views.

Good news. You have leverage here. At some point in the beginning, your teens will not have a device and will want you to get them one. Use this to your advantage. This is a natural window for an earnest conversation about what they post, share, and send and what that could mean to their future.

Don't fret. Even if your teen already has a cell phone, it's likely that you as the parent purchased that device for them. And you likely pay for their cell phone plan. And they live in your house. And they were the reason you were in back labor for seventeen hours.

Don't be timid here. Remember that a teenager having a cell phone is not an inalienable right protected by Article 4 of the US Constitution.

What to Do

1. **Help your teen realize that this is their public résumé.** Future colleges, universities, and employers will look at your teen's digital imprint, and they will make decisions based on that. In a recent survey, 77 percent of employers reported using search engines to learn about potential candidates. And of those researching candidates online, 35 percent eliminated a candidate from consideration based on information they uncovered online.

The interview doesn't begin when you walk through the door for that face-to-face meeting. It begins when the employer types your name into Google.

Try saying this: "As crazy as this sounds, you are going to want to have money in order to be an independent adult, and you're going to need a job for that. Your future employer will google you. So think about what you're posting because it could cost you your future job. And you don't want to have to live with me forever."

2. **Teach them the "grandma filter of approval."** Helping teens think more critically about what they post on the Internet is a crucial aspect of self-governance, and one way to promote this is to introduce the concept of a self-filter. The idea is to allow teens to pause, breathe, and think critically about what they post or send. A good way to do this is to introduce a memorable question through which they can filter their decisions. My favorite is "Would my grandma be okay if I posted this?" Of course this assumes that their grandma isn't a foulmouthed, chain-smoking racist who's down with the 420 life. But if their grandma is a prototypical sweet grandma, they should be fine.

Try saying this: "Before you post something online, ask yourself, 'Would I be cool with Grandma seeing this?' Would Grandma be happy to see you threatening to beat up that kid you don't like? Would Grandma be impressed with you uploading a picture of yourself in front of the bathroom mirror wearing only a sports bra? It's a helpful way to think about what to post and what *not* to post."

3. **Teach your teen to THINK before they post.** There's an old Quaker story called "The Three Sieves" about a boy who runs home to tell his mother about a rumor he has heard. She stops him midsentence and tells him to run his story through the three sieves of truth, kindness, and necessity to "strain out" whether the story merits retelling. The mother's advice holds true for us in our digital age.

Here's a helpful acronym (a modernized three sieves, if you will*) to help your teens filter their content and learn to think critically about what they post online:

---

* And we will.

T—Is it **true?** There is so much misinformation out there, and so much just plain *wrong* information out there. Before you spread info (whether it's a news article or information about a peer), make sure that info is accurate.

H—Is it **helpful?** Is what you're saying practical and productive? Don't be like the Internet trolls who post things often for the sole reason of being mean. The opposite of "helpful" would be "harmful" or "injurious," so stay away from that. Also, in case you're wondering, cat videos *are* helpful because they bring rays of pure sunshine into the world.

I—Is it **inspiring?** Words have the power of life and death. What effect will the words you say and type today have on the people around you? Make sure that your words breathe a little bit of life into someone's day, give hope, advance understanding, and encourage others.

N—Is it **necessary?** Just because you *can* say something doesn't mean you should. Sometimes it's best to bow out and not post anything. Just because someone is throwing an insult party or riling things up online, that doesn't mean you have to attend or participate.

K—Is it **kind?** The tone of so much of the Internet is cruel. Do your part to reverse that. As Sir Ken Van Meter famously said, "There are two ways to say a thing. One of them is kind." Make sure you take the "kind" way.

NOTE: We've created a snazzy little poster you can download* and print to help create awareness with the young people in your life. Perhaps you could hang this stunning piece of art above the common area where your computer resides.

---

* Head to joshshipp.com/ggtth to download the THINK poster.

Helping Them Understand the Harmful Effects of Pornography

Special thanks to Clay Olsen, founder of Fight the New Drug, a nonprofit whose goal is to educate youth about the harmful effects of pornography, who was consulted to address the nuances of this topic.

The Challenge

We live in a time when teenagers deal with pornography to an extent and to a scale that no other generation has ever had to deal with. It's no longer an issue of if your teen will encounter pornography, but when. It used to be that the only pornography available to teens was old copies of Uncle Russell's *Playboy* magazines stored in the basement. Now pornography is ubiquitous. The rise of the Internet in our modern age has provided for an unprecedented expansion and distribution of pornography into our world. One of the world's largest adult sites says that it gets 2.4 million visitors per hour and that in 2015 alone, people around the globe watched 4,392,486,580 hours of its content—4.39 trillion hours.

Here's what we know: A huge percentage of adolescent boys and girls are highly interested in sex and therefore in pornographic content. A smaller percentage begin viewing this material and become unable to think about almost anything else. And an unknown percentage of these young boys and girls begin to believe that what they are seeing in pornography is normal sexual behavior.

The following are actual responses from actual teens when asked the question "What do you wish your parents knew when talking to you about the issue of pornography?"

> *"I wish my parents understood that shaming me only led me to hide it."*
>
> *"I wish my parents would address the issue personally and not sweep it under the rug."*
>
> *"I wish they knew that it's not always controllable and that we want to change but that sometimes we're just stuck and we don't know who to turn to or how to reach out."*

In our modern world, dealing with pornography has become a central issue in adolescent development.

Your Goal

Talk about pornography with your teens, help them understand its effects, and give them the tools they'll need to navigate through the porn-filled online world.

What to Expect

Trust your parental instincts. Watch out for the warning signs of suspicious Internet behavior. If your teens start skipping meals, staying up late, locking the door to their bedroom, routinely deleting their browser history, or offering convoluted or shaky explanations for online behavior—you ought to talk.

And you'll need to talk about this sooner than you wish. The average

age that someone is exposed to pornography is nine years old. As soon as your child has access to the Internet, you need to start having age-appropriate dialogue about sex and pornography.

For younger teens and preteens, consider keeping computers in the common areas of the home. This will help you monitor and keep tabs on the content your teen is viewing. Many parents install blocking programs or filters, but no system is 100 percent foolproof.

Try sharing a line like this: "If you see anything that's seems inappropriate to you, please come and tell me." Let your teens or preteens know that they won't be in trouble. You simply want to work to make sure those images don't show up while they're on the Internet.

If your teen is struggling to stop watching pornography, you can help. Because of the wet-cement neuroplasticity of the teenage brain, recovery is not only possible but likely. For example, I've sat with many young men as they tearfully described how much they wanted to stop visiting porn sites. For each of these young men it led to the point where they could think of little else. For each of these success stories, breaking free started by openly talking about the issue and then brainstorming and taking deliberate steps to put systems in place (like utilizing filtering software, putting computers in public areas only, and setting up daily check-ins with mentors). These steps allowed them to be successful.

In these sorts of situations, you must stay away from shame. And helping teens see that some things are wrong without making them feel like *they* are wrong is tough. Even if you know your teen has been watching pornography, you have to be careful how you handle the conversation. Your teen probably feels guilt, which is the psychological discomfort people feel when they do an inner assessment and hold up something they've done against their own values. In those cases, guilt is a good and instructive emotion. It helps us realize we shouldn't do whatever makes us feel that way. But shame is different. Shame is an awful feeling, the belief that something is wrong with you and that you're unworthy of love and connection. It's not helpful. Teens are inherently—biologically—interested in sexuality. It's part of their development. And mixing shame with sexuality always produces a bad cocktail, so be careful in your language and framing when you approach them about porn.

And please note: Your teen will absolutely not want to have an in-depth conversation with you. If you've discovered that your teen has been looking at porn, it's highly unlikely he or she will want to sit down and talk things through. In this superawkward scenario, it's good for many parents to have a short introductory talk* to break the ice and set up a future conversation (details to follow on that). Your teen may not say much, but he or she will think about what you said.

What to Do

If you suspect your teen has viewed pornography, psych yourself up to have a crucial conversation. If you don't talk to teens about this sort of stuff, they will get their information from other, less trusted sources. And make sure you are prepared to have this talk before jumping in or they will pummel you. Consider this Abraham Lincoln quote: "Give me six hours to chop down a tree and I will spend the first four sharpening the axe." Once you are prepared, pick a time that makes sense and a place that's private to have this conversation.

Open by saying this: "As you know, one of our rules around technology is that I will periodically check what you're looking at online. I've noticed from your history that you have visited some adult sites. I'm not here to embarrass you, but I want to make sure you understand some of the risks associated with this material. You can expect this incredibly awkward conversation to last about eight minutes."

---

* Followed by a short introductory shot of tequila.

TALKING POINT #1: THE LURE OF PORN CAN FEEL
OVERWHELMING. LET ME EXPLAIN WHY.

Facts you (the parent) should be aware of: Watching pornography is an escalating behavior that can lead to addiction. Your teenager—along with every other human on earth—has a cluster of nerve cells in the middle of the brain called the nucleus accumbens. This "pleasure center" releases chemicals that make people feel good when they do something rewarding, like eat a great meal or win a competitive event. The problem is that this pleasure center can be tricked and hijacked. When teenagers are aroused by porn, their brain releases a chemical called dopamine that makes them feel pleasure. As the dopamine goes through their brain, it leaves behind a pathway that connects the feeling of arousal to looking at porn, basically saying, "This feels good; let's remember how to get back here." The more teens look at porn, the more those pathways get wired into the brain, making it easier and easier for them to turn back to porn, whether they want to or not. This is not unlike drug addiction.

Say this to your teen: "Sex is a natural, biological instinct and it produces incredibly strong desires. It can awaken very powerful feelings. There were times growing up when I felt like I was powerless to it. Like I was being controlled by a tractor beam. But part of growing up is thinking deeply about these feelings, and that means making sure you start thinking with other parts of your body."

What this communicates: You should seek to think clearly about your own sexual desires and feelings. Also your sexual desires should not be the primary controller of your behavior.

Be appropriately vulnerable.[*] Share a story from your own life about these sorts of perplexing sexual desires. Did you ever give in to these feelings in a way you regretted? How did you learn to manage them?

---

[*] If your idea of "appropriately vulnerable" begins with the words "You know, your mother and I . . ." kindly invite your teen to tase you.

Just so you know, this will be supremely awkward. For the mental health of your teen, don't focus on the details, but instead focus on what you learned.

TALKING POINT #2: PORN PORTRAYS SEX IN A WAY THAT DISTORTS ACTUAL HEALTHY SEX.

Facts you (the parent) should be aware of: In real life, real love requires a real person. Pornography showcases sexual expression without any of the very real and human aspects of human sexuality. And one of the central problems of pornography is that it helps provide teens with what researchers call a "social script" for how human sexuality is supposed to work. The problem is, this script is deeply flawed. Pornography has a common script: the only needs to be considered are the sexual needs of the man. Pornography is objectification taken to its extreme, and it presents the idea that love does not have to be built on mutuality and respect. In reality, a porn habit can take a serious toll on people's ability to offer someone real, unselfish, meaningful love—which often means that in the end, they're left without much more than what's behind that screen.

Say this to your teen: "Here's my fear. My fear is that watching these videos will give you the idea that this is what real sex is like. And I'm older than you, so I can say this: Sex doesn't work like that. Sex in pornography is about using people for their bodies. But that's not what healthy sexuality is. Healthy sex is never about exploiting someone just so you can get what you want. It's about affection and love and sharing and connecting."

What this communicates: Healthy sex never takes, steals, or exploits. Pornography doesn't represent healthy sex, which is actually about connecting and sharing and giving.

Be appropriately vulnerable: Talk about a time when you saw sexuality misused to hurt or exploit someone. And talk about healthy sexuality that you've seen and experienced.

TALKING POINT #3: LET'S TALK ABOUT STEPS WE CAN TAKE TO HELP.

Facts you (the parent) should be aware of: As a parent, you can use technology to your advantage. Obviously, you want to help your teenager choose a healthy approach to sexuality instead of pornography. That's most important. But it's not a bad idea to show your teen how to install and use filtering software that blocks certain types of adult content. It's sort of the same principle behind not stocking Doritos in the house if you're trying to be healthy: because you don't want to have a weak moment and eat the whole bag. Additionally, installing accountability software—software that acts as a log and sends a report to you of what websites your teen visits—can be a good way to encourage good decision-making.

Say this to your teen: "As part of our technology agreement, we've agreed that we won't watch pornography. I want you to think about how we can make this happen, together."

What this communicates: We can make good decisions while we are in our right mind.

Be appropriately vulnerable: We encourage you to install accountability or filtering software on your own phone and computer (to show your teen that it's your value, too). Using filtering software to block objectionable content at the router for your home shows your teen that you're serious about not wanting this type of content in your house— for anyone. And don't forget that a teen's phone is leverage—so talk to them about this issue before you give them a phone, and make sure that not viewing pornography is an agreed-upon value.

Extra Credit Talk: What Is Healthy Sexuality?

Instructions: Use these discussion questions one at a time to begin to have conversations with your teen about healthy sexuality and relationships. These questions are designed for you to practice listening with empathy to your teenager's actual thoughts about human relationships and sex. They will also hopefully allow you to ask different follow-up questions to see what your teenager believes. Finally, in a conversational setting, these questions could lead to a situation where you have the chance to clearly articulate your experiences and values and how you arrived at them. If this is done in a way that doesn't directly shame or threaten your teen, it could lead to positive interactions.

- Besides physical attributes (cuteness, handsomeness), what other factors or characteristics do you think are most important right now for you in a person you'd want to date?
- When you think about your future husband or wife, what characteristics do you want them to have? What is most important to you, if you had to make a list right now?
- Based on your life experience, what do you think are the two most important components of a fantastic long-term relationship or marriage?
- Sex is an aspect of relationships. What do you think are the two main benefits of sex in a relationship?
- Have you ever heard about a situation where sex was not a good thing and resulted in something really damaging happening to someone?
- What do you think is the difference between "healthy" sex and "unhealthy" sex?
- Thinking about your own life and your friends, where do you think most teenagers learn about sex?
- We live in a sex-saturated society that's very different from when I was growing up. In what ways do you think that affects your peers or your generation?
- Pornography is widely available today. Do you feel that this has a negative impact on your generation in general? Why or why not?
- What do you think most teenagers would say the most difficult or confusing thing about sex is?
- What is something that confuses you about sex?

Helping Them Deal with Cyberbullies

Special thanks to Dr. Dion Metzger, professor in psychiatry at Emory University School of Medicine, Medical College of Georgia, and Morehouse School of Medicine, who was consulted to address the nuances of this topic.

The Challenge

When you were growing up, the stereotype of a bully was a school yard bruiser who demanded that you hand over your lunch money—or else. In fact, even the most famous cultural bullies fit into a certain mold in the popular imagination. Whether it's the mean-spirited, barb-throwing elitism of Draco Malfoy in the Harry Potter series, the towering selfishness of Biff Tannen from the *Back to the Future* trilogy of films, or even the simple, leather-jacket-clad thuggishness of Moe from *Calvin and Hobbes*, the primary unifying thread for most adults is that bullies do their work in the physical realm: with threats, words, pushes, and punches.

And it's true that back in Biff's 1955, most bullying was physical. But this is *not* the way bullying works for most teenagers today. Only about 20 percent of all bullying done by teenagers today is physical.

The vast majority? Cyberbullying.

This doesn't mean that physical and verbal bullying has vanished from schools everywhere. We deal with this issue separately, in the final section of the book.

The chances of your teen experiencing cyberbullying are very high. Roughly 52 percent of all teenagers say they've been cyberbullied, and 95 percent of teens that witnessed bullying on social media say they ignored the behavior.[26] But ignoring it does not make it go away.

Your Goal

Help your teen process cyberbullying and arm them with strategies for dealing with digital antagonists.

What to Expect

There's a reason that there has been a dramatic rise in cyberbullying. It's just psychologically easier. You don't have to look the other person in the face. Plus if the cyberbullying is done through an anonymous account, this further emboldens teens to be mean.

Teens also cyberbully because they don't consider how their actions will negatively affect another person. Teens, by their very nature, act on impulse. The part of their brains that tempers those impulses (the prefrontal cortex) hasn't fully developed. So while adults often think about the aftereffects of bullying (how it would make someone feel), teenagers often don't have enough life experience to do this. This, coupled with the fact that digital antagonists rarely see the effects of their online comments on the person they bully, creates a classic case of out of sight, out of mind.

Your teen will likely internalize a cyberbully's comments. When children are little and something is said about them, they often go to their parent to see if the assessment is accurate. "Mommy, so-and-so said I was stupid." What you say as a parent carries mammoth amounts of weight during these years. But as children grow and become aware of the social voices and influences in their world, the way they are seen by other people grows in importance. So when teens are cyberbullied, they are highly likely to internalize the insults. The reasons for being bullied reported most often by teens were looks (55 percent), body shape (37 percent), and race (16 percent). Your job is to try to help your teens see that they didn't do anything wrong and that nothing is wrong with them. Bullies often just wander around picking on everyone until they get a reaction. It's highly likely your teen has been bullied for nothing more than existing.

What to Do

1. **Do NOT minimize what happened, and do NOT blame them.** Online bullying often entails a large audience. For your teen, it's the emotional difference between being bullied in the locker room after gym class and being bullied on a microphone in front of the whole school at an assembly. Don't minimize the fear, anxiety, and shame that your teen might feel. And be aware that the psychological tendency of teens after an incident of cyberbullying is to shift the blame to themselves. Don't accidentally add to their shame and embarrassment by suggesting it's their fault. This will feel like punishment to your teen, and they will regret telling you about what happened.

2. **Help your teen understand what cyberbullies are going for: a reaction.** Bullies want attention, and the most common reaction of teenagers is to respond back and return an insult—the "You hurt me, so I'm going to try to hurt you back" way of thinking. But if you can, coach your teens to see that if they don't take the bait, the bullies won't get what they want and will move on. This has to be coached, because if your teen, in a moment of anger or hurt, lashes back, it can quickly become a turf war, and the bully will recruit others to pile on, resulting in the fulfillment of his or her objective: a reaction.

3. **Show them how to block the jerks.** If someone is bullying your teens, teach them how to immediately block that person out of their

social media circle.* This is especially important if your teen doesn't even know or have an actual relationship with the bully. You can find helpful resources on the various social media platforms that will give you step-by-step instructions for how to block someone.

4. **Teach your teen which voices to dial up and dial down.** If it's true that cyberbullying chips away at teenagers' positive self-image, then they're going to feel under siege when this happens (and this won't be the last time). Teach them what to do when they feel this way. At times like these, it's critically important to identify a handful of trusted people (both peers and adults) to be the source of feedback. This feedback should be both positive ("you have an incredible sense of humor") and critical ("occasionally when you're in a new situation, you can act annoying"). Say something like this: "Look, you're under attack from people who frankly don't even know you. So you need to intentionally dial up the voices of the people who do. Let's make that list of those people."

5. **Intervene immediately if there's a threat of bodily harm.** As an adult, you *must* respond if there has been a threat made of bodily harm. It can be vague ("I'm going to kill you") or specific ("I will come over to your house and shoot you"). Do not dismiss this as idle talk. File a police report AND report the incident to the school authorities. You must take these words seriously.

6. **Suggest counseling.** Ask your teen this question: "Would it help if you had somebody else to talk to about this?" If your teen says anything even close to yes, then take him or her to counseling. Although we're completely biased, we think counseling is fantastic. It gives teens a clear ally and an outside source of support. It helps teenagers find a guide to help them sort through feelings of false shame and guilt. And it allows teens to find their own voice and identity.

---

* This will also prove helpful when they grow up and innocuously post a comment wondering if it makes sense for dogs to wear sweaters, only to be viciously attacked for being an "anti-dog-warmth fascist."

THE STATE OF THE TEENAGE UNION: BULLYING

MOST COMMON TYPES OF BULLYING[*]

- Taunting (66 percent)
- Name-calling (66 percent)
- Laughed at (44–49 percent)
- False rumors (36–42 percent)
- Physical (24–29 percent)

More than 90 percent of kids are online by grade three.

PERCENTAGE OF KIDS WITH THEIR OWN CELL PHONES[27]

- Grade three: 20 percent
- Grade five: 30 percent
- Middle school: 83 percent
- High school: 86 percent

CYBERBULLYING DATA[28]

- 10 percent of all middle schoolers have had "hate terms" hurled against them.
- 11 percent of adolescents and teenagers reported that embarrassing photographs were taken without their knowledge.
- 25 percent of teenagers report that they have experienced repeated bullying via their cell phone or on the Internet.

---

[*] Stats, figures, and research provided by the Massachusetts Aggression Reduction Center (MARC).

- 55 percent of teenagers who use social media say that they have witnessed outright bullying via that medium.
- 52 percent of teenagers report that they have been cyberbullies.
- 20 percent of teenagers say they experience cyberbullying regularly.
- 50 percent of teenagers say that they never confide in their parents when cyberbullying happens to them.
- 88 percent of teenagers say they have witnessed their peers being cruel or mean to others.
- 33 percent of teenagers who reported cyberbullying incidents against them reported that the online bully issued threats.
- 95 percent of teenagers who witnessed cyberbullying ignored the situation.

The Long-Term Effects of Bullying

Bullying hurts everyone involved. Both the victims of bullying and the bullies themselves have a much higher risk of psychiatric disorders in adulthood.[29]

VICTIMS

Subject to anxiety disorders at a rate 4 to 5 times higher than average.

BULLIES AND VICTIMS

Subject to depression at a rate 4 times higher than average.
Subject to anxiety disorders at a rate 18 times higher than average.
Subject to suicidal tendencies at a rate 18.5 times higher than average.

BULLIES

Subject to antisocial personality disorder at a rate 4 times higher than average.

Cyberbullying, Decoded

Flaming: An intense and aggressive argument that normally takes place on social media, over instant messages, or via email. Often it can involve multiple people ganging up on one person to humiliate them or drown them in an aggressive, cruel, or mocking comment stream.

Impersonation: This is an elaborate form of cyberbullying in which bullies pretend to be someone they aren't by either creating fake email addresses (or social media accounts) or by using someone else's email, phone, or mobile accounts to cyberbully another person. This method protects the actual identity of the real bully.

Cyber stalking: The repeated use of electronic communications to harass or frighten someone—for example, by sending threatening emails. Social media and messaging gives stalkers new opportunities to contact, follow, and harass their victims.

Outing: The public display (or forwarding) of private personal communications such as text messages, emails, or instant messages. The public posting of content intended to be private and the dissemination of this information can be very damaging socially.

Trolling: This word is drawn from a fishing term and refers to a hook and line drawn through the water behind a boat. Trolling is where someone posts deliberately offensive or provocative material online for the sole purpose of upsetting others or eliciting an angry response from them.

FADE IN: *EXT. A SINGLE-FAMILY HOME—THURSDAY AF-TERNOON AROUND 2:30 p.m.*

DISSOLVE TO: *INT., FAMILY ROOM*

MOM, an earnest woman in her midfifties, elegant and upright.

DAD, soft around the middle, with a salt-and-pepper beard.

MARCUS, their son, a nineteen-year-old wearing tattered jeans and a T-shirt that reads "Scruffy Looking Nerf Herder."

DAD: So why are we here?

MOM: Marcus, you're making me nervous. You sounded so serious on the phone.

MARCUS: (*A little nervous*) Well, Mom, Dad. I have something to tell you.

DAD: This can't be good.

MOM: Did you get a girl . . .

MARCUS: No! Just listen, okay? This might be a bit difficult to hear.

MOM: Ohhhhkay.

MARCUS: I hate my college.

MOM: You hate college?

MARCUS: The problem is not that the work is too academically difficult. It's that I hate it.

According to college counselors, the primary reason that students don't succeed in college is not academic preparedness. The two top reasons given are vagueness about long-range goals or inappropriate choice of major.

MARCUS: And because of that, I'm not doing well this quarter. At all.

DAD: You're not doing well?

MARCUS: No. In fact, I'm failing.

DAD: Failing? Do you know how much money college costs? Last year I spent $22,000 on your tuition alone. I could be driving a BMW with that kind of money.

MOM: Honey.

DAD: I mean, your mother could be driving a BMW with that kind of money.

MOM: (*Gives Dad a look that could kill*) What your father is trying to say is that college is very, very expensive.

MARCUS: I get it. It's your money. I get that. But I think there's a reason I hate school. Dad. You told me that your first year of college, you just floundered through school.

MOM: That's true.

MARCUS: You started off majoring in Communications. Which basically means you don't know what you want to do.

DAD: Exactly.

MARCUS: That's where I am right now.

FEAR:
Many parents are afraid that their children will repeat the same mistakes they made—the ones that made life extra difficult for them.

MARCUS: So I'm going to drop out of college.

DAD: Oh my God. You're going to move back in, aren't you?

MARCUS: No! Dad!

DAD: I just turned your room in the basement into my man cave.

MARCUS: (*Trying to get a word in edgewise*) Uh, Dad . . .

DAD: I got three fifty-five-inch TVs. I can watch three games at once!

MARCUS: But, Dad!

DAD: (*Pleading, to his wife*) Don't let him take my man cave away.

MARCUS: Dad! I'm not moving back home.

FEAR:

Parents are afraid that their children will not reach financial independence, since living on one's own is a key benchmark of being a responsible adult.

DAD: (*It's sinking in*) Do you mean it?

MARCUS: Yes. I promise.

DAD: I am so happy. I thought you were moving back in.

MOM: James! Honey, you are always welcome . . .

DAD: To visit.

MARCUS: Dad, I get it. I promise, I will not move back into your house. Ever.

DAD: Good. Well.

MARCUS: And if you see me trying to move back in, you have permission to lock the door and pretend like you've moved away.

MOM: Honey, we would never . . .

DAD: No, I would do that. Pull the drapes, lock the doors. I'm okay with that.

MARCUS: Can we get back to college, please?

DAD: Yes. Okay.

MARCUS: I'm likely going to drop out.

DAD: Drop out? Drop out.

MOM: Oh, honey.

MARCUS: Let me explain my plan. I will enroll at another college next spring, and in the meantime, I'll work as an aide at

Lark Spring Elementary. And I'll also get a job on weekends working at the children's hospital in town.

MOM: What will you do there?

MARCUS: I actually have it lined up. It's perfect.

DAD: What is it?

MARCUS: Well, I'll be spending time with children in the hospital who are waiting for bone marrow transplants or other serious medical procedures, and I get to work with them by cheering them up, talking with them, telling them jokes.

MOM: Does the hospital provide that service?

MARCUS: No. It's a nonprofit.

MOM: What's the program called?

MARCUS: It's called Clown Care.

DAD: Clown Care?

MOM: Like, you'll be a clown?

MARCUS: Yep.

DAD: With red noses and juggling?

MARCUS: Yep.

DAD: Great. Looking forward to those conversations. (*Pretending to be talking to someone else*) "So, how's Marcus doing at college?" "Well, ummm, he dropped out to be a clown."

FEAR:

Many parents fear their children will make choices that won't turn out well, and as a result, they will be viewed as failures as parents. They think that their children's choices will be a referendum on them as people.

MARCUS: Dad, you and Mom have been great parents. If I had to go back and choose anybody on earth to be my parents, I'd choose both of you instantly.

MOM: (*Touched*) Oh.

MARCUS: But I need to go out there and try. So I'm going to transfer. And I'm going to change majors.

DAD: To what?

MARCUS: I'm going to get my degree in teaching and be a special education teacher.

MOM: Oh.

DAD: Special education?

MARCUS: Yes. I want to work with kids with autism.

DAD: You're going to work in the public school system as a special education instructor?

MARCUS: Yes.

DAD: That can't pay well.

MARCUS: Dad, it's like this. Remember when Mom had that sports hernia?

MOM: Yes.

MARCUS: So what was it that made you comfortable with the doctor, Dad?

DAD: The man was knowledgeable. He had done this procedure a hundred times. He was clearly competent.

MARCUS: How would you have felt if he said, "I'm only here because my parents wanted me to be a doctor. And I really don't care about this or any other procedure. It's tedious and boring to me."

DAD: Uh.

MARCUS: Exactly. And Dad, that's how I feel about computer science. I hate it.

DAD: What? I thought you liked it. You got such good grades in math in high school.

MARCUS: I think part of growing up is figuring out what you're supposed to do with your life.

MOM: Well, how do you know this is what you want to do?

MARCUS: Good question. So this semester we had to do thirty hours of community service. And I went into a local elementary school and got to do read-aloud workshops with these students in a special education class. They're all autistic, with learning disabilities. And I don't know—I just loved it. And that thirty hours turned to two hundred and eighty. The teacher kept inviting me back.

> A good indication that you're in the right job or doing
> the right thing is if you keep doing it voluntarily.

DAD: Well, of course she did. Free help.

MARCUS: No, it was more than that. The teacher said that I had a knack with these kids. And I loved hanging out with them and they loved me. There was just something about connecting with those kids and helping them "get it" . . . you know?

MOM: I do.

MARCUS: Before all that, I didn't even know what autism was. Or that there are real ways you can help connect with these kids. It was just . . . I don't know. I feel like it's my thing.

DAD: Right.

MARCUS: So I'm going to work hard and help some kids. I'm going to trust that the money will take care of itself.

DAD: That . . . makes sense.

MOM: I think it's wonderful. Sometimes it takes much longer to find your calling.

MARCUS: I feel the same way. And if I end up falling on my face, if anybody tries to blame you, you tell them to come and talk to me. Because this is my choice. So put your mind at ease. You won't get any blame for this.

DAD: You won't fail, son. I know you.

MOM: This makes you happy?

MARCUS: Yes.

MOM: Then go for it.

MARCUS: Thanks, Mom.

DAD: And you can come over any time for dinner. But if you try to move in . . .

NARRATOR: Few things are more worrisome for parents than the thought of their teen walking unprepared into the future. Here are some helpful tips about how you can have meaningful and helpful conversations about school, their career, and life.

How to Think About School and Education

Special thanks to Dr. Joe Martin Jr., award-winning teacher, trainer, and author of *Tricks of the Grade*, who was consulted to address the nuances of this topic.

The Challenge

Jeff graduated sixteenth in his high school class of six hundred. His grades were good enough to earn him a full scholarship to Southern Methodist University in Dallas, where he figured he'd follow in his dad's footsteps by majoring in engineering. But Jeff didn't have a great engineering mind and got straight Cs in the courses for his major.

Soon Jeff realized he was pretty good at something else—business. He excelled there, so he switched majors and became a stellar student. After graduating from SMU, Jeff applied to the most prestigious MBA program in the nation (at the Harvard Business School), and during his admission interview, when asked why the school should admit him, Jeff simply said, "I'm f**king smart."

Well then.

But Jeff wasn't wrong. He got his MBA and graduated in the top 5 percent of his class from Harvard. He was snatched up by the nation's premier consulting firm, where he became the youngest partner in the firm's history.

Let's pause right here. Right now, Jeff's story is pretty much every parent's dream, right? I mean, except for swearing during his admission interview at Harvard, maybe. Your kid gets into a good school, then a great school, then moves up the ladder, achieving prestige, power, and wealth. This is the American Dream, is it not?

The American Dream Narrative

You go to school to get good . . . grades
You get good grades so you can get into a good . . . college
You get into a good college so you can make lots of . . . money
You make lots of money so you can buy lots of . . . stuff
You buy lots of stuff so you will be . . . happy

But this narrative can easily come apart. Let's go back to the story of Jeff. Jeff was moving on up. He then caught the eye of a big shot (the CEO of one of the largest companies in Texas) who immediately hired him. It was the late nineties and the US economy was kicking. Jeff realized that if he could make it seem like his company was making tons of money, people would buy stock in his company and everyone would get rich.

In 2000, Jeff told everyone the company made $979 million. But really, the company had lost $1.2 billion. That's a big difference. And with that, the seventh largest company in the world . . . went bankrupt.

That man? Jeff Skilling. That company? Enron.

It was the greatest corporate fraud ever committed in the history of the United States. Almost all 20,600 Enron employees lost their jobs, and many lost every dime in their corporate retirement accounts. Enron's stock price went from $83 to 67¢ nearly overnight, losing trusting investors $63 billion.

And Jeff Skilling was sentenced to twenty-four years in prison.

How did things go so wrong? Jeff Skilling was educated by the best schools and universities in the United States. And that educational system—the best in the world—created a brilliant businessman. But it did not produce a brilliant AND ethical businessman.

In the end, it wasn't Jeff's education that failed him. It was his character.

Jeff Skilling's life shows us in clear relief that even the very best education, absent character formation, can result in suffering.

Your Goal

Use your wisdom and insight to skillfully play the role of career counselor for your teen.

What to Expect

College graduates make more money. According to the 2012 data provided by the US Census Bureau, the idea that education opens doors for jobs and careers with far more opportunity for advancement and financial compensation is generally accurate.

EDUCATION	AVERAGE EARNINGS
Not a high school graduate	$20,457
High school graduate	$31,429
Some college, no degree	$33,119
College degree	$57,762
Master's degree	$73,771
Professional degree	$127,942

That being said, college graduates have more debt. In the past twenty-five years, the average amount of student debt has climbed almost 300 percent. This can cripple graduates with significant financial problems. As of 2016, here are the numbers:

- 70 percent of college graduates borrow money to finance higher education.[30]
- The median amount of college debt in 2016 was $37,172.[31] (In 2012, it was $26,885. In 1992–1993, it was $12,434.[32])
- Last year, there was $1.26 trillion in total US student loan debt.[33]
- 44.2 million Americans shoulder student loan debt.
- The rate of student loan delinquency is 11.1 percent.[34]
- The average monthly student loan payment[35] (for borrowers age twenty to thirty) is $351.

It's a real possibility that without proper guidance, your teens could get into a situation that could burden them with intense debt for decades, limiting their career options, limiting their freedom, and setting them up for failure.* Because of the dramatic increase in cost, higher education is now like a lightsaber: You gotta know what you're doing or you'll end up killing yourself.

What to Do

1. **Do NOT waste $100,000.** If you were going to invest $100,000 in stocks, you would probably do your due diligence to make sure that the company you were thinking of putting your money into was healthy and had a good business model. And yet many parents send their kids off to college without helping their primary investment— their teens—figure out how to best use their gifts. Most college students change their major four or five times because they go into college blind, without much forethought about their career or themselves. This is a very expensive form of try-and-see career counsel-

---

* I read an article in the satire news website *The Onion* whose headline captured this sentiment perfectly. It read, "Failure to Get Into Private College to Be Most Financially Responsible Act of 17-Year-Old's Life."

ing. A recent study by the University of Texas found that students drop out of college because (1) they have vague goals about the future, and (2) they picked a major they were ill suited for. Don't let this happen to your teens. You have their future (and a lot of money) riding on this.

2. **Play the role of career counselor.** As a parent, you are in the best position to be a career counselor for your teens because you've seen their strengths, their weaknesses, and their gifts. You know what makes them come alive, what they enjoy, and what makes them cry. You know what their personalities are like. Do the hard work of helping your teens make sure they're not vague about their future and that the major they pick is right for them. Professions and careers aren't simply jobs—they're callings, unique to the distinct shape of our kids.

3. **If you're paying for your teen's college, then you have input.** If you're paying for your teen's college education, then you have a right and an obligation to make sure he or she has a real shot at being successful in a career that is not only meaningful but can eventually pay the bills. Being a theater major at UC Irvine might be exciting, but telling your moderately talented teen that his or her dreams of making it big on Broadway are a long shot (at best) seems cruel. Who wants to be a crusher of dreams, after all? However, there's a difference between being a dream-crusher and being rooted in reality. If your teens want to pursue dreams you feel they are ill suited to accomplish, try to help them see that with kindness and truth. And if you can't change their mind, don't feel any obligation to foot the bill for college.

4. **Don't try to raise successful college graduates.** As the illustration about Jeff Skilling shows, education is a tool, but it doesn't create the person. Education is a massively important aspect of realizing human potential, but it's not the end goal. Think about it this way. Try to raise excellent future husbands and wives and fathers and mothers. Raise children whose future spouses and children will say of them, "If I had a do-over and I got to choose, I would want them as my father/mother/ spouse all over again."

How to Help Your Teen Find His or Her "Calling"

If you are serious about helping teens find their calling and a career they will love, here's what you can do.

STEP 1: Gather the data points.

The first step in this process is preparation. Answer the following questions about your teen. Then ask for input from a few other trusted adults who know them well.

- What do they love?
- Since they've been little, they have always _____.
- What three adjectives best describe them?
- What are things they hate and want to make right?
- What kinds of things have they actively pursued with no real prompting from anyone else?
- What can they do for hours without growing tired of it?

STEP 2: Have your teen do a self-assessment.

Set some time aside and have your teen assess himself or herself based on the following questions:

- I love the following things . . .
- Write down three adjectives that best describe you. Why did you choose these adjectives?
- Please write down something that makes you absolutely furious. Why does this bother you so much?
- What is an area in life where you've had a lot of success and positive feedback from leaders?

- Talk about a time in life when you were doing something that made you feel alive. What were you doing? Explain the environment and situation.

STEP 3: Talk about it.

With your teen, review the information gathered from you, other caring adults, and the teen self-assessment. Answer the following questions together:

- What was most interesting to you about what other people said about you?
- What common ideas emerged?
- What questions did this process bring up that it didn't answer?
- What did this exercise reveal to you? What did you learn from this activity?

At the end of that meeting, bring out Step 4.

STEP 4: Do a weeklong marinade.

Give your teen a sheet of paper with this question on it. Have him or her sit with the question for an entire week. Say that in seven days, as a family, you are going to talk about this:

If you knew that you couldn't fail, what is the one thing that you would attempt to do with your life?

STEP 5: Have a conversation about the answer to the question.

Try to reserve all judgment. The next step will do a lot of the heavy lifting for you. For example, if your teen has a terrible idea for a career, the next step will help correct your teen's errant thinking.

STEP 6: Hand out an interview assignment.

Have your teen locate three passionate people in the field they identified and interview them face-to-face. By "passionate," I mean people who love what they do.

INTERVIEW QUESTIONS

- What qualities, interests, and experiences did it take for you to get this career?
- What path did you take educationally and in your career to get here?
- If you could go back, what would you do differently?
- What's the best advice that you would have for someone who is interested in entering this field?
- What are the best books to read for people interested in entering this field?
- What is your favorite part of this job?
- What part of this job do you hate?

STEP 7: "Test-drive" the job.

After your teen completes the interviews, have him or her learn more about that job or career by volunteering to work for free at that job or spending a day shadowing someone doing it.

- Take immediate action. Get a résumé together, along with a cover letter explaining what you're trying to get out of this internship and what your skills and experience are.
- Send your materials and cover letter to the person you interviewed and ask for their help procuring an unpaid internship. Explain your goal: You're interested in this career and would like to know more about it from the inside.

- Ask what you can do to help the company, and make it clear that you want to add value to the company. And because you're not getting paid, it's a good deal for the company.
- Emphasize flexibility. Because interns often serve to fill in the holes in businesses and offices, there sometimes aren't clear job descriptions, just a general "gofer." Make it clear you're ready to do whatever needs to be done.
- Say you're ready to start immediately. This shows hustle and flexibility.

STEP 8: Review and evaluate.

After your teen has completed the time volunteering or job-shadowing, sit down and have a conversation about the experience.

- What did you learn from this experience?
- What surprised you most about this career that you didn't know?
- Knowing what you know now, do you feel that anything has changed?

At the end of the day, every parent says that they just want their teen to be happy. But that's not the whole picture. You also want your teen to grow up to be a person who has a positive impact on the world. Who uses his or her unique talents and passions to make a difference. In the end, we'd be wise to follow the advice of writer and theologian Frederick Buechner, who once wrote, "Your calling is the place where your deep gladness and the world's deep hunger meet."

How to Help Your Teen Succeed in the New Economy[*]

Special thanks to Dr. Robert B. Kozma, emeritus director and principal scientist for the Center for Technology in Learning at Stanford Research Institute (SRI) International, who was consulted to address the nuances of this topic.

The Challenge

The River Rouge Complex in Detroit was a marvel of manufacturing. More than a mile and a half long and a mile wide, it contained its own power plant and water supply. Raw iron ore went in one end and completed automobiles came out the other end.

From 1900 through the late eighties, that River Rouge Complex was like a social mindset. Because with manufacturing, certain key values are critical. Values like standardization. Precision. Efficiency. Things have to be mass-produced at a high level of precision, and all

---

[*] Of course by the time you're reading this book, the "new economy" could very likely have transformed into something else, mainly because of the new robot overlords. Kidding. Gulp. Hopefully. Though these cycles are complex, it's good to be thinking about the shifting trends when helping your teen think about a future career.

the parts have to work together. So you want all your workers to know the same things and the same procedures.

In a real way, manufacturing shaped our entire culture and ethos as a people. It leaked into everything. It was a cultural mindset. And because employers wanted certain types of workers, our educational systems and universities produced them. Employers (like Ford) wanted someone who knew how to do what needed to be done and who effectively followed the protocols. Things like creativity weren't valued at all, unless you could be creative in making things more precise or in making production faster and more efficient.

But then things shifted.

Fifty years ago, the highest valued companies in the entire world were manufacturing companies. Now a large majority of the most valued companies in the world are technology companies.

Because our economy is shifting from manufacturing to technology, the new cultural paradigm is based on creativity, innovation, and novelty. This has implications for everything and everyone, including your teen.

This new economy has new rules. And you need to know what those new rules are to help your teenager navigate through them.

Your Goal

Help your teen be prepared for success in the new economy.

What to Expect

With all the changes in our economy, there remain three key areas that robots will likely never be able to improve upon. These areas provide distinctly human advantages.

THE MODERN ECONOMY WANTS WORKERS
WITH CREATIVITY AND INNOVATION.

What's valued today is being able to create new ideas, new services, and new content. This involves various ways of thinking. For example, just take a look at the Apple app store. It's up to app developers to figure out what people want, what would be helpful or fun or useful, and then create that app. And it's very democratic: Almost anybody—if they have the appropriate skill and some access to technology—can produce something new. And with any luck, profitable.

THE MODERN ECONOMY WANTS WORKERS
WHO CAN COLLABORATE.

The new technology economy is more like a theater company than an assembly line. There is a real need for someone to come in, listen to, say, three perspectives, and then use his or her gifts to synthesize those ideas and perspectives into a fourth perspective that would not have existed otherwise. In this way, leadership in the technology economy is not about telling people what to do and getting them to produce the way it is in a manufacturing economy. Instead, it's about building coalitions who trust one another to solve the most complex problems.

THE MODERN ECONOMY WANTS WORKERS
WHO CAN SOLVE COMPLEX PROBLEMS.

The modern workforce needs more and more people who can understand complex systems and identify potential creative solutions. Think about a company such as Uber. They saw a problem and figured out a creative way to solve a transportation issue, by in essence monetizing the empty spaces in people's personal vehicles. If you thought about the problem from a manufacturing mindset, the only solution would be to make more taxis or make the taxi routes more efficient. Our global problems are many, and they will require incredibly nimble and creative solutions.

What to Do

1. **Help your teen practice synthesizing information.** In the information age, it's important to help your teens understand how to evaluate sources of information. Help them see potential bias ("What does this source have at stake on this issue?") and the veracity of the information ("What data is this information based on? What's the source? Is this fact or opinion?").

2. **Put your teen in team situations.** Parents can also help their teens develop social knowledge, a crucial skill that is not overtly part of the curriculum in most schools. Social knowledge is built up in any situation where teens have to collaborate and work together. Sometimes there are after-school programs where kids work on science projects or creative works. The essential part of group work is bringing in different skills and perspectives to do something one person couldn't do otherwise.

3. **Play tabletop games. Seriously.** There's been a renaissance of late in tabletop gaming, and many of these award-winning games include well-thought-out scenarios that teens have to work together to solve. Whether it's honing their precise communication skills (in Codenames), frantically problem-solving (in Pandemic), collaborating to unearth clues to a massive puzzle (in Mysterium), or strategizing in rapidly changing and deadly scenarios (in Flash Point), these tabletop games not only activate your teens' imaginations and brains, but require teamwork and communication. This will pay dividends later when your teen plans the family's optimal path through Disneyland. But more important, teens will build skills today to help them be effective employees in the future.

4. **Look for real-world projects that connect education to real life.** Parents can also help connect school knowledge with real-world knowl-

edge by drawing connections from school subjects to kids' everyday lives. It's great to look through an educational lens for projects around the house you can do together. For example, let your teenager plan your family camping trip. Where will we go? What will we need? What is our food budget? What's the history behind the location? What stories will we share around the campfire? Turn it into a math problem, a geography problem, a history lesson, or a creative writing prompt. Planning for this type of camping trip* is an excellent chance to rehearse the type of problems your teen will have to deal with in the workforce. There will be challenges with complex variables and very real consequences that require various types of planning and skills to navigate through.

5. **Help your teen take ownership of his or her own education.** Parents can make a big difference by helping teens take ownership of their own education. Supposedly this is taught in high school, but honestly, it's just not part of the curriculum. Help your teens plan their own learning. What is important to them? What do they want to learn this next semester? What do they want to learn and accomplish educationally this next month or week? And then, what resources do they need to be successful, and how can you help? Kids are hardly ever asked this; they expect the teacher to tell them what they have to learn. But teaching your teens to take ownership over their learning empowers them and helps set them up for future success. It's a crucial role that parents can play in their kids' lives.

---

* Also, there might be a bear. Your teen must be prepared to shoot and field-dress it and harvest its meat. This skill will prove effective in almost any modern workplace. Apologies for this footnote. I just watched *The Revenant*.

How to Respond to a Bad or an Unfair Teacher

The Challenge

At some point, your teens are going to come to grips with the uncomfortable reality that they are not in complete control of certain aspects of their life.*

As you've learned, part of growing up means understanding what it means to have an authority figure in your life. For instance, you know what it means to have a boss. Your boss has power over your life and over certain areas of your well-being. They can change your job description, transfer you, or even fire you.

Your teen already has these sorts of bosses, just with different titles. Coach. Principal. Shift manager. And if it's true that your teenager is a developing human, then school is their "job" and their teachers are their "bosses." Helping your teen navigate through those completely unbalanced power dynamics and dealing with a variety of authority figures is a crucial part of life.

Sometimes that process is easy and rewarding. And sometimes—just as in the grown-up world—your teen will have to deal with a bad

---

* They already sorta know this because you made them give up every other Saturday morning to take piano lessons with Mrs. Takano, who smelled like elderberries and Vicks VapoRub.

boss, in the form of a difficult coach or an unfair teacher. Here's how to set them up for success in these unfortunate scenarios.

Your Goal

Empower your teens with practical strategies to deal respectfully with an unfair authority figure so that when they inevitably encounter another one, they'll be prepared.

What to Expect

You'll be tempted to solve the problem. It's natural: You hear that your teen is having an issue with a teacher, and you want to march in and set things right. But you can't go to the gym for another person. You must help train your teen how to deal with unfair (and even awful or incompetent) authority figures with maturity and wisdom. Part of growing up is figuring out how to handle your problems, including problems with people in authority. It's better for teenagers to handle tough situations and learn from the experience than have someone do it for them.

Think about how frustrated you become with unfair, mean, or incompetent bosses. It's maddening.* Your teen will be just as upset, only without the filter, maturity, and tact of a fully formed adult brain. You have to help your teen calm down and see exactly what is going on. Then give them a script for how to de-escalate the issue and solve the problem. It often helps to give teens specific words to say in certain circumstances, and they should rehearse this conver-

---

* At the end of a particularly bad day with his boss, my friend Matt told me he was "pondering the merits of homelessness."

sation before having it. This will give them confidence and a game plan. It might not work, but at least your teen will have tried—and will have been prepared.

Beyond that, the only time you must get involved and take action is if what your teen is saying about a teacher or authority figure encompasses behavior or actions that are illegal or unethical, result in legitimate safety concerns, or are physically, verbally, or emotionally abusive. Your teen could be exaggerating or blowing things out of proportion, but it's now up to you to investigate and raise the flag to the appropriate school or local authorities.

What to Do

There are three major types of bad or unfair teachers—here's how to handle each.

TYPE #1: The teacher is unprepared and/or disorganized.

Teachers like this frustrate their students with a lack of preparation, unclear assessment strategies, and poor communication of clear learning goals.

Your teen will say things like "I don't know what we're even doing in this class" or "we don't learn anything in this class" or "the test had nothing to do with what was covered in the class" or "I don't even know how I got the grade I have."

The Strategy: Overcommunicate
Coach your teen to cleverly (and respectfully) force the teacher's hand to be more organized and clear. Have your teen set up a time to meet privately with the teacher to figure out what the teacher expects. During this meeting, teens should write down upcoming projects and homework for which they will be graded and should ask the teacher

for information on what steps they can take to ensure they complete the learning goals of the class. Don't use language like "I want to improve my grade" but rather "I want to make sure I do everything you expect of students in your class."

Talking points for your teen: "I want to succeed and I want to work hard in your class. But sometimes I am not clear about what is expected of me. What assessments are coming up, and how could I best prepare myself so that I will succeed? Perhaps you could help me write out a list?"

TYPE #2: THE TEACHER IS UNFAIR AND/OR PLAYS FAVORITES.

Such teachers sap educational enthusiasm by unequally enforcing class rules.

Your teen will say things like "I got in trouble for something I didn't do" or "I didn't even do anything" or "He/she is not fair" or even use the words "He/she plays favorites."

The Strategy: Humility

Coach your teens to make their case privately in a winsome way that will disarm the teacher. The first step in this is to approach the teacher privately. Confrontations in front of the class never work. Also, if your teens feel unfairly singled out for punishment or think that a teacher's policy is tacitly unfair, teach them to discuss the matter with humility by apologizing, affirming, and then clarifying. For example, let's say your teen was given detention for eating Halloween candy in class (in violation of class rules) because a wrapper (that was not theirs) was found beside their desk. Your teen would likely protest in front of the class, which would cause the teacher to feel threatened. The teacher would then likely "dig in" and get more rigid. And now all communication is shut down, and your teen is endlessly frustrated.

Talking points for your teen: Use the words "I agree" and employ "I" statements. First, affirm the teacher's right to make the rules. "I agree with you that eating candy in class is not a good idea. I agree that's a good class rule. And if I'd broken that rule, I would agree with the detention. But that's not what happened." Also, use "I" statements. Instead of saying, "You're an unfair teacher," which will put the teacher immediately on the defensive, say, "I feel like I didn't have the chance to explain to you that I wasn't breaking the rule. And I feel that it's unfair to get detention when I didn't eat any Halloween candy."

TYPE #3: THE TEACHER IS MEAN AND/OR DISRESPECTFUL.

Such teachers treat students as subordinates or use their position of authority to disrespect the personhood of a student.

Your teen will say things like "That was totally uncalled for" or "I can't believe they said that to me" or "I refuse to be in a class with that teacher anymore" or "He/she is just a terrible person."

The Strategy: Mature Conflict Resolution

Coach your teen to be the bigger person. If your teen is locked in a passive-aggressive battle of wills with a teacher, he or she can be the one to stop the cycle. This will take a great deal of maturity, but have your student approach the teacher, begin the process of apologizing, and request a time to meet privately. It's important that your teen own up to his or her part of the tension (even if the teen is only 1 percent wrong and the teacher is 99 percent wrong, the teen must take 100 percent responsibility for that 1 percent).

Talking points for your teen: "I respect your authority and want to get along in this class. Did something I say or do come across as disrespectful to you?" This will show that your teen is willing to listen, which will dramatically increase the chances that the teacher will listen. Listening and respect usually beget listening and respect. Then coach your teen that when airing grievances, he or she should use the phrase "I feel like it was unfair when . . ." Give specifics and explain why what the teacher said came across as disrespectful, while being as honest as possible.

Respectfully Confronting a Teacher: How It Might Play Out

FADE IN: *EXT., A HIGH SCHOOL—THURSDAY AFTER-NOON AROUND 2:30 p.m.*
DISSOLVE TO: *INT., CLASSROOM*
MR. SEILHAMER, *a teacher who is standing in front of a whiteboard and a large desk covered with papers, looks up.*
Many students sit in desks around him, including JORGE, a black-haired sixteen-year-old.
A bell rings.

MR. SEILHAMER: Okay, gang. That's it. Turn in your work, and we'll see you tomorrow.
JORGE: (*Waiting for the students to file out of class*) Thanks for agreeing to meet with me after school.
MR. SEILHAMER: No problem.
JORGE: I wanted to talk to you about the research paper.

> **WHAT THIS COMMUNICATES:**
> By requesting a private meeting, you show that this issue is important to you (because you're giving up your free time to discuss this). The private setting also allows the teacher to let his or her guard down. This is NOT a challenge to their authority in front of the classroom.

MR. SEILHAMER: The one that was due today?
JORGE: Yes. That's the one.

MR. SEILHAMER: The one you have yet to turn in?

JORGE: Yes.

MR. SEILHAMER: The one that's worth 15 percent of your grade?

JORGE: Yes. First off, I wanted to apologize for not turning it in. I knew it was due. I didn't get it in. That's on me.

> **WHAT THIS COMMUNICATES:**
> Apologizing is disarming. It shows humility.

MR. SEILHAMER: It sure is.

JORGE: I understand your rule about deadlines.

MR. SEILHAMER: No late submissions.

JORGE: And I agree with the principle behind that rule. I guess it teaches us to be responsible.

> **WHAT THIS COMMUNICATES:**
> By agreeing with the teacher that deadlines are in general important, you disarm the teacher. And they are more likely to agree with something *you* say later on.

MR. SEILHAMER: Yes.

JORGE: I'm not trying to be lazy. I'm not trying to get out of work or anything like that.

MR. SEILHAMER: Well . . .

JORGE: If you look at my track record, that's what you'll find. I don't turn in my work late.

> **WHAT THIS COMMUNICATES:**
> Explaining how your past behavior shows compliance.

JORGE: I have my paper mostly done. Is there any chance I could submit my research paper the day after tomorrow?

MR. SEILHAMER: Well, if I make this exception for you, I have to do it for everyone.

JORGE: Can I explain to you why I did not get my paper done, Mr. Seilhamer? This is not an excuse, but a reason.

> **WHAT THIS COMMUNICATES:**
> Everyone gets defensive with the word "excuse." But a reason is an explanation of why something happened.

MR. SEILHAMER: Go ahead. I don't know if it will make a difference.

JORGE: Well, it will to me. You see, my little sister is in competitive gymnastics. And she was competing in the regional competition this past weekend. Our whole family went to cheer her on, and she did very well and advanced. So what I thought was going to be a six-hour competition ended up being a fourteen-hour competition. I simply ran out of time.

> **WHAT THIS COMMUNICATES:**
> Being honest about your reasons gives your teacher a chance to empathize.

MR. SEILHAMER: Well, you knew about this assignment weeks ago, Mr. Moreno.

JORGE: I did. And I planned on using this weekend to finish the paper. But sometimes things don't go as we planned. Right, sir?

> **WHAT THIS COMMUNICATES:**
> Everyone knows that sometimes life gets out of control and things happen that we didn't anticipate. You're simply reminding the teacher about this reality.

MR. SEILHAMER: That is true.

JORGE: I didn't get the paper done. It's my fault. But I will get it done. And you and I won't have a conversation like this ever again.

> **WHAT THIS COMMUNICATES:**
> By taking complete responsibility as Jorge did and promising that this won't be a pattern, you will defuse your teacher's main fear that this will become a continuing issue.

MR. SEILHAMER: Okay, Mr. Moreno. Just turn your paper in by tomorrow by sixth period.

JORGE: Thank you for your flexibility.

Helping Them Deal with Bullies

Special thanks to Dr. Keith Berry, cochair of the National Communication Association's Anti-Bullying Task Force and author of *Bullied: Tales of Torment, Identity, and Youth*, and Dr. Sameer Hinduja, codirector of the Cyberbullying Research Center, who were consulted to address the nuances of this topic.

The Challenge

There's an old saying, "A parent is only as happy as their least-happy child."[36] And if your teens are being bullied, teased, mocked, or purposely excluded, then they are going to be unhappy—and that affects you.

They're not alone: Six out of ten students say they've witnessed bullying at least once per day. And according to the National Center for Education Statistics, the reasons for being bullied reported most often by students were looks (55 percent), body shape (37 percent), and race (16 percent). Bullying is an unfortunate reality for teenagers.

But what if I told you that the most common parental gut instincts about bullying are both right *and* woefully incomplete?

It's natural to be upset about bullying. That anger you feel is justified: Cruelty shouldn't have a place in this world. But your most common reaction is almost always incomplete. And therefore the solutions offered by adults to teens are often lacking.

Here's what I mean: Nearly all of the research and antibullying efforts in our nation's schools focus on creating safe environments. And rightfully so. This is of course a very good thing. In the past several years, schools have focused on implementing antibullying programs and initiatives, and in general, these have been very successful. In fact, school-based bullying prevention programs decrease bullying by up to 25 percent.

This is fantastic, but if your kid is being bullied, then it's not that helpful.

Because—and this is tough to hear—adults can never create and maintain a world for teenagers that is perpetually friendly, compassionate, kind, and uplifting. Sadly, we are not Willy Wonka.

Creating safe, bully-free environments is crucial. But there's a missing piece that adults really need to bring to the table. In addition to creating safe environments, you need to, as a caring adult, help build resilience in your teen.

Because at the end of the day, bullying is NOT a school problem. It's a human nature problem.

And although we want to, we can't completely rid the world of bullies or cruel or rude people. You've been in a parking lot at the mall during the holidays, right?

Most of us can remember a moment when we were bullied, often recalling incredibly specific details and even words. (For me, it was "No wonder your parents left you.") These moments can haunt us. It would be wise for us to lean in when our teens have one of these moments.

Because if you are intentional, you can help build resilience in your teens so that bullies and emotionally charged peer conflict do not exert an out-of-proportion emotional toll on them. This will not be the last cruel and out-of-line person they'll have to deal with throughout the course of their lives. But you can give your teens tools that will help them process bullying emotionally and move forward.

Your Goal

Cultivate resilience within your teens and help them develop social competencies so they can deal with hate and believe they are capable of solving their own social and relational problems.

What to Expect

WHAT EXACTLY IS BULLYING?

It might be helpful to have a formal definition. Here's what we know about bullying from social scientists who study this kind of thing:

- Bullying is always a deliberate behavior (there's no such thing as accidental bullying).
- Bullying is a behavior that's repeated over time.
- Bullying always occurs where there is a power imbalance between two people. This power differential could be physical (strong vs. weak), relational (popular vs. not as popular), emotional, or psychological.
- This power imbalance almost always means that the victim is less likely to defend him- or herself.
- Bullying is an aggressive act done to chip away at the positive self-concept of another person.

But in the end, definitions—even precise ones like this crafted by social researchers—aren't really worth debating. The bottom line is impact. Is your teen affected negatively by the purposeful words and actions of another teen? Then you should look into it.

BULLYING LEADS TO ANXIETY.

Repeated exposure to bullying affects teens' brains because bullying causes anxiety, and anxiety leads to elevated cortisol levels. When the level of this hormone is high, a teen's memory is affected dramatically, making even something as simple as remembering a homework assignment challenging. There is a definitive correlation between bullying and achievement. Students perceived as poor performers or unmotivated may be actually unable to complete work on time or understand material being taught.[37]

YOUR TEEN IS WAITING TO SEE IF YOU WILL BE HIS OR HER ALLY.

Parents should be careful not to ignore or dismiss stories of their teens being bullied. Their antennae are looking for what communication theorists call disconfirming messages, which are messages that minimize the story and the person that's telling the story. This can happen in subtle ways, like when an adult says things like, "Well, what did you do to him?" or "Why didn't you stand up for yourself?" These messages are critiques, and teens will read them as such. Your teen has already gone through the process of being minimized by the bully—he or she doesn't need to experience it again. You're dealing with an emotional teenager, and whether or not this story turns out to be perfectly accurate, the point is that the story is a bridge to finding out what's actually going on.

What to Do

1. **Teach your teen that suffering is a part of life.** Most cultures— unlike our own—see suffering as an inevitable aspect of life and a means for enriching one's experiences and strengthening one's character. You can help teens understand that suffering is something we all go through, and that they should expect obstacles and even hate

from some people. But that doesn't mean that life is drained of its meaning: It means that they have a chance to live a great story. Every great character in every great work of art has to overcome some obstacles. If it helps, you can even use examples of characters from one of their favorite movies or books to help your teens see this perspective.

2. **Use your own life stories of resilience.** What are some examples in your own life where you overcame some tough obstacles? Share those stories. You think your kids will roll their eyes, but they will not. When you share that your grandparents came over to the United States from another nation and worked hard to build a small business, it shows your teens that they are a part of a story about resilient people. And that helps give them the courage to be strong and push through, just like their mom or grandpa did. Say something like this: "Can I tell you about a time when I felt really humiliated?" Or "Is it okay if I share with you a story from my own life where I faced a pretty tough obstacle like the one you're facing?"

3. **Utilize lateral activities that will build resilience.** If you look at old cathedrals, they were feats of engineering. Their height was possible because of the load-bearing buttresses along their sides that strengthened them. In the same way, you can build strength in your teen to stand up and be resilient to bullies by participating in activities that develop the muscles of perseverance and hard work. Hike that trail that's difficult, and then hike it again carrying a twenty-pound backpack. Complete a 5K race, and then sign up for another race together. Figure out, day after day, how to solve a Rubik's Cube using online instructions. Whenever teens push themselves (or are pushed) beyond what they thought they could do, it strengthens their minds. They are given a clear data point on themselves, and they can say, "Yeah, I did that. I am a resilient person." Consider something they'll enjoy or want to do that is also quite difficult, and then go do that.

4. **Teach your teen which voices to dial up and which to dial down.** I purposely suggest this again because although the ways bullying and cyberbullying play out are different, the emotional effects of both on your teens are similar. It chips away at their self-concept and makes

them feel under siege. Teach them what to do when they feel like they're under siege. At times like these, help them identify a handful of trusted people (both peers and adults) to be the source of feedback. This feedback should be both positive ("you have an incredible sense of humor") and critical ("sometimes when you're in a new situation, you can act annoying"). Say something like "Look, you're under attack from people who frankly don't even know you. So you need to intentionally dial up the voices of the people who do. Let's make that list of those people."

5. **Intervene immediately if there's a threat of bodily harm.** As an adult, you simply *must* respond if there has been a threat made of bodily harm. It can be vague ("I'm going to kill you") or specific ("I will come over to your house and shoot you"). Do not dismiss this as idle talk. Make a police report AND report the incident to the school authorities. You must take these words seriously.

6. **Suggest counseling.** Ask your teen this question: "Would it help if you had somebody else to talk to about this?" If your teen says anything even close to yes, then take him or her to counseling. Although we're completely biased, we think counseling is fantastic. It gives teens a clear ally and an outside source of support. It helps teenagers find a guide to help them sort through feelings of false shame and guilt. And it allows teens to find their own voice and identity.

THE STATE OF THE TEENAGE UNION: BULLYING

- Almost one out of every four students (22 percent) reports being bullied during the school year.[38]
- Six out of ten students say they've witnessed bullying at least once per day.
- The reasons for being bullied reported most often by students were looks (55 percent), body shape (37 percent), and race (16 percent).
- 40 to 75 percent of most bullying incidents occur during class breaks, in the cafeteria, in bathrooms, or in hallways.[39]

- 30 percent of students with food allergies are often taunted or threatened, having the allergen thrown or brandished at them.
- 57 percent of the time when a peer intervenes in a bullying situation, the bullying tends to stop within ten seconds.[40]
- The percentage of students who experience a bullying incident in school in grade six = 39 percent.
- The percentage of students who experience a bullying incident in school in grade twelve = 20 percent.

In a survey of 14,000 high school students, the most common types of bullying were the following:

- Taunted = 66 percent
- Name-calling = 66 percent
- Laughed at = 44–49 percent
- Rumors = 26–32 percent
- Physical = 24–29 percent[41]

Students named the most common reasons[42] other students are bullied:

- Their body size/appearance (36.2 percent)
- Actual/perceived sexual orientation (19.2 percent)
- Race/ethnicity (10.4 percent)
- Academic ability (10.1 percent)
- How masculine or feminine they are (9.2 percent)

Percentage of students who experienced the following types of bullying:

- Bullied at school = 21.5 percent
- Made fun of, called names, insulted = 13.6 percent
- Rumors spread about them = 13.2 percent

- Pushed, shoved, tripped, or spat on = 7.4 percent
- Excluded from activities on purpose = 4.5 percent
- Threatened with harm = 3.9 percent
- Pressured to do something they did not want to do = 2.2 percent
- Property destroyed on purpose = 1.6 percent[43]

Some types of bullying are illegal.

The Department of Education sends out memorandums to all public schools reminding school leaders and administrators that some student misconduct that falls under a school's antibullying policy also may trigger responsibilities under one or more of the federal antidiscrimination laws enforced by the Department of Education's Office for Civil Rights due to the Civil Rights Act of 1964. To quote the DOE, "School districts may violate these civil rights statutes and the Department's implementing regulations when peer harassment based on race, color, national origin, sex, or disability is sufficiently serious that it creates a hostile environment and such harassment is encouraged, tolerated, not adequately addressed, or ignored by school employees."[44]

IN CLOSING: **YOUR VOICE MATTERS MORE THAN YOU KNOW**

The *New York Times* published a story about a father who was walking down the streets of East Hampton, New York, with his preteen daughter. This father began to hum and sing to himself, and his daughter, mortified by this, turned to her father and pleaded, "Daddy, please don't sing."

That man? Billy Joel.

Indeed, the same Billy Joel who has sold out Madison Square Garden thirty-two times so people could *hear Daddy sing*. But to his daughter he is not six-time Grammy Award–winner Billy Joel. He is simply the most embarrassing dad in the entire world.

Now, this is fantastic news for us as parents, because it means that it's not just *your* teen who doesn't recognize your brilliance.* But here's the thing you have to know: Just because you grasp this intellectually doesn't make it hurt any less.

Right now your teenagers are going through a lot. They are in that difficult stage of life where they're trying to figure out who they are and how they are different from you. And so they roll their eyes. And

---

* I mean, if Billy Joel's daughter doesn't want to hear him sing . . . am I right?

sigh. And make verbal jabs. We all did this. Didn't you? It's almost a rite of passage.

But if we aren't careful as parents, we can begin to buy into these mixed messages that seem to say, "Go away!" And that hurts. You and I both know that parenting is a crucible that no one told you about, filled with tears and angst and laughter. It is all those things.

And for all your effort, here's something I can practically guarantee. Being a parent is often a thankless job. Nobody hands out awards to good parents. You won't be mentioned during the state of the union address. There won't be a lifetime achievement award given to you at the Academy Awards.

So why put yourself through all this? Because that's what you do when you love someone.

You change their diapers.

You rock them back to sleep after a nightmare.

You help them with their math homework.

You listen when their heart gets broken.

You hold their hand at the funeral.

Because that's what love does.

Even when your teens' confusing signals say otherwise, your voice is the single most important voice in their lives. And in those moments when they're honest with themselves, your teens instinctively know that they need your voice.

So be like Billy Joel. Keep singing. Because your voice is needed and crucial and matters more than you know.

Just. Keep. Singing.

Thanks for doing what you're doing. It's an honor to have met you in these pages.

RESOURCES FROM JOSH

THE SEVEN THINGS EVERY TEEN NEEDS TO HEAR

According to a recent study published in *Science* magazine, adults say about 16,215 words per day.

Here are seven phrases—each one less than five words—that every teen needs to hear from you, regardless of their age or stage.

1. **I love you.**

    This is crucial. Always be strong enough to say this to your kids. Grown adults have told us they have *never* heard this from their parents. If your teen doesn't hear it from you, I don't know whom he or she will hear it from.

2. **I'm proud of you.**

    As parents or caring adults, it's important we applaud effort more than achievement because achievement is often subjective to the group we are competing against. So applaud and reward effort over achievement and let your child know you're proud of him or her.

3. **I'm sorry.**

    Taking responsibility as an adult is important for our kids to see. We have to model what it looks like to be an adult and apologize when we make mistakes. And don't cop out by saying, "I'm sorry, but . . ."! Remember that kids learn a little bit from what we say, a little more from what we do, but the most from who we are.

4. **I forgive you.**

It's crucial for young people to know that if you want to succeed, you must be willing to fail. They are going to screw up—it happens. The question is always this: What will you do when they inevitably mess up? When you say, "I forgive you," kids know it's okay to admit mistakes.

5. **I'm listening.**

Once your child is a preteen or teen, the name of the game isn't about control—it's about influence. You can't control a fifteen-year-old, but you can influence him or her by listening and asking questions. Lecturing doesn't work as well as asking strategic questions and then listening; doing that will help teens come to their own mature decisions and beliefs about situations.

6. **This is your responsibility.**

Don't bail your kids out of problems they can solve. Instead, remain like a coach: Prepare them before the game, cheer from the sidelines, and then review what went well and what went badly (also from the sidelines). The urge is there because we care, but stay off the field! If you fix it for them, they'll interpret that to mean that they don't have what it takes. Instead, be there for moral support and guidance, but let them take responsibility.

7. **You've got what it takes.**

It's important for them to hear from you that they have what it takes. If they know you believe in them, they're better prepared to take baby steps to accomplishing their goals and dreams and facing those difficult situations.

Bonus:

8. **No.**

Sometimes the most loving and caring thing you can tell a kid is no. Rest assured, they won't always appreciate it in the moment. But years later, they will circle back and praise your brilliance. If we say no to the things that are wrong, it allows us to say yes to the things that are right.

TWENTY-ONE WAYS TO ASK YOUR TEEN "HOW WAS SCHOOL TODAY?" WITHOUT ASKING THEM "HOW WAS SCHOOL TODAY?"

Used with permission from Elizabeth Evans, cofounder of Simple Simon and Company.

1. What would your school be better with? What would your school be better without?
2. If you were a teacher, what class would you teach?
3. What was the coolest (or saddest, funniest, scariest) thing that you saw today?
4. What's *one* thing that you learned today?
5. If your day at school was a movie, what movie would it be?
6. Who do you think you could be nicer to?
7. Which is your easiest class? Which is your hardest class? Which class are you learning the most in? Which class are you learning the least in?
8. If you could read minds, which teacher's mind would you read?
9. If today had a theme song, what would it be?
10. Which class has your favorite group of students in it?
11. What do you think you should do more of at school?
12. What are the top three things that you hear people say in the halls?

13. What do you think the most important part of school is?

14. If an alien spaceship landed at your school, who would you like them to beam aboard and take back to their home planet?

15. Who did you help today? Who helped you today?

16. What part of the day do you look forward to? What part of the day do you dread?

17. What would you change about school lunch?

18. Which classmate is most likely to be arrested, made president, become a millionaire, be in movies, let loose a flock of wild chickens in the library, etc.?

19. If you had to go to only one class every day, which class would it be?

20. If your day at school was an emoticon, which one would it be?

21. What do you think your teachers talked about in the faculty room today after school?

FORTY-TWO WAYS TO CONNECT WITH YOUR TEEN

1. Take them out to lunch with no agenda.
2. Take them to an unexpected event they'll enjoy.
3. Write them a handwritten card. Special occasion not required.
4. Send weekly random encouraging text messages.
5. Care about what they care about.
6. Tell them you're proud of something meaningful you saw them do.
7. Attend their events—athletic, band, theater, debate.
8. Teach them a proper handshake.
9. See their annoyances as assets in disguise.
10. Acknowledge family hardships quickly and openly.
11. Apologize quickly and openly when you screw up.
12. Ask them what their favorite movie is and then watch it with no judgment.
13. Ask them what they see themselves doing in the future.
14. Involve them in an important decision.
15. Create family times around specific activities they've told you they enjoy.
16. When dealing with irritating/chaotic/moody teen behavior, ask yourself, "What are they really trying to say?"
17. When you catch them doing something good, praise them publicly.

18. Schedule specific slots of time every week for time together.

19. Ask open-ended questions that build critical analysis: "What would you change about your school to make it better?"

20. Acknowledge their fear as real, even if you don't agree with it.

21. Watch an important documentary and discuss.

22. Talk about the lives, accomplishments, and even failures of extraordinary people. Ask them who they admire and why.

23. Make a list of ten things you admire about them and give them the list.

24. Encourage them to read important self-development books.*

25. Point out an example in the news of someone who was compassionate.

26. Have regular one-on-one chats on important topics that are quick. Start by saying, "Let's discuss something tricky. You can expect this to last five minutes."

27. Ask what worries them the most about their future.

28. Keeping inviting them even if they say no.

29. Talk to their friends, learn their names, and be their advocate.

30. Volunteer at a local nonprofit together. This builds appreciation and perspective.

31. Ask what their favorite song is, listen, and look for deeper meanings beyond the sound and lyrics.

32. Eat together on a predictable schedule (for example, every Sunday night).

33. Don't belittle them in front of their friends.

34. Ask their opinions about political drama in the news.

35. If you can, travel with them. Let them pick a destination.

36. Celebrate *effort* more than results.

37. Follow through on promises, no matter how small they seem.

---

* Head over to joshshipp.com/ggtth to see my list of "Eighteen Books Every Teen Should Read Before They Turn Eighteen."

38. Schedule times to talk about unappealing topics if they're not coming up naturally.
39. Plan some random one-on-one time as a complete surprise.
40. Go watch a stand-up comedian or funny movie.
41. Ask them for help on something that really matters.
42. Pick a tricky recipe and cook something together.

THE LETTER YOUR TEENAGER CAN'T WRITE YOU (YET)

Used with the permission of Gretchen Schmelzer, PhD, a licensed psychologist trained as a Harvard Medical School fellow and author of *Journey Through Trauma*.

Dear Parent:

This is the letter that I wish I could write.

This fight we are in right now. I need it. I need this fight. I can't tell you this because I don't have the language for it and it wouldn't make sense anyway. But I need this fight. Badly. I need to hate you right now and I need you to survive it. I need you to survive my hating you and you hating me. I need this fight even though I hate it too. It doesn't matter what this fight is even about: curfew, homework, laundry, my messy room, going out, staying in, leaving, not leaving, boyfriend, girlfriend, no friends, bad friends. It doesn't matter. I need to fight you on it and I need you to fight me back.

I desperately need you to hold the other end of the rope. To hang on tightly while I thrash on the other end—while I find the handholds and footholds in this new world I feel like I am in. I used to know who I was, who you were, who we were. But right now I don't. Right now I am looking for my edges, and I can sometimes only find them when I am pulling on you. When I push everything I used to know to its edge. Then I feel like I exist, and for a minute I can breathe. I know you long for the sweeter kid that I was. I know this because I long for that kid, too, and some of that longing is what is so painful for me right now.

I need this fight and I need to see that no matter how bad or big my feelings are—they won't destroy you or me. I need you to love me even at my worst, even when it looks like I don't love you. I need you to love yourself and me for the both of us right now. I know it sucks to be disliked and labeled the bad guy. I feel the same way on the inside, but I need you to tolerate it and get other grown-ups to help you. Because I can't right now. If you want to get all of your grown-up friends together and have a "surviving-your-teenager support-group rage fest," that's fine with me. Or talk about me behind my back—I don't care. Just don't give up on me. Don't give up on this fight. I need it.

This is the fight that will teach me that my shadow is not bigger than my light. This is the fight that will teach me that bad feelings don't mean the end of a relationship. This is the fight that will teach me how to listen to myself, even when it might disappoint others.

And this particular fight will end. Like any storm, it will blow over. And I will forget and you will forget. And then it will come back. And I will need you to hang on to the rope again. I will need this over and over for years.

I know there is nothing inherently satisfying in this job for you. I know I will likely never thank you for it or even acknowledge your side of it. In fact, I will probably criticize you for all this hard work. It will seem like nothing you do will be enough. And yet, I am relying entirely on your ability to stay in this fight. No matter how much I argue. No matter how much I sulk. No matter how silent I get.

Please hang on to the other end of the rope. And know that you are doing the most important job that anyone could possibly be doing for me right now.

Love,
Your Teenager

TEEN CELL PHONE CONTRACT

Dear Parent,

This contract is designed to create an open line of communication between you and your kids regarding their cell phones. The goal is to help your kids become well-rounded people who can coexist with technology, not be ruled by it.

You probably find yourself in one of two situations:

Situation #1: They already have a cell phone with no clear rules in place.

Expect the conversation to be a bit tougher here. They will feel you are setting the ground rules after the game has begun. Admit that you made a mistake (we all do) and you're doing this because you care about them (which you do).

Situation #2: You're about to give them a cell phone.

GOOD NEWS! There is no better time to get people to agree to what you want than when you're handing them a shiny new toy. "I just need you to review and sign this understanding about your cell phone—then it's all yours!"

*Next, feel free to edit the contract as needed to make it your own.**

Encourage your kids to ask questions, and don't be afraid to have a few laughs along the way.

Cheers,
Josh Shipp

---

* At joshshipp.com/ggtth you can download an editable/customizable version of this contract.

Dear _____,

CONGRATS! *You've proven yourself mature and responsible enough for your own cell phone. Given that you have a new cell phone in your hands, we obviously trust you to make good decisions—so why are we making you sign this lame thing that's loaded with stuff that you probably already know?*

Well, let me get to the point.

A cell phone is more than a piece of technology. If used incorrectly, it can be a weapon that puts your safety at risk. You've always been a great kid, and we want to make sure that you continue making smart choices.

The goal of this agreement is to make sure that you're always safe and happy—and that we always maintain a direct and open line of communication. I'm asking you to always use your phone for good and to ask for help from me or a trusted adult when a situation leaves you feeling scared or unsure.

Please review this contract, and be sure to ask me any questions that you may have.

With love,

_____

CELL PHONE AGREEMENT

1. I understand that the rules below are for my safety and that my parents love me more than anything in the world. I understand that my parents want to give me freedom, while also giving me enough security to make smart choices.
Initial here: _____

2. I promise that my parents will always know my phone passwords. I understand that my parents have a right to look at my phone whenever there's a need for them to do so, even without my permission.
Initial here: _____

3. I will hand the phone to one of my parents promptly at _____ P.M. every school night and every weekend night at _____ P.M. I will get it back at _____ A.M.
Initial here: _____

4. I will not send or receive naked photos. Ever. I understand that there could be serious legal consequences that could put my own and my parents' futures at risk.
Initial here: _____

5. I will never search for porn or anything else that I wouldn't want my grandma finding.
Initial here: _____

6. I understand that my behavior on my phone can impact my future reputation—even in ways that I am not able to predict or see.
Initial here: _____

7. I will tell my parents when I receive suspicious or alarming phone calls or text messages from people I don't know. I will

also tell my parents if I am being harassed by someone via my cell phone.

Initial here: _____

8. When I'm old enough, I won't text and drive. I understand it's dangerous and stupid.

Initial here: _____

9. I will turn off, silence, and put my phone away in public— especially in a restaurant, at the movies, or while speaking with another human being. I am not a rude person. I will not allow the phone to change this important part of who I am.

Initial here: _____

10. I will NEVER use my phone to bully or tease anyone, even if others think it's funny.

Initial here: _____

I understand that having this phone is not a right—it is a privilege that can be taken away. As such, I have read the following document and agree to the above rules. I understand that if I have any questions, I should ask.

_____

(Sign here)

WORK WITH JOSH

Here are three ways you can access additional resources and insights from me and my team:

1. **Sign up for video training and our newsletter for parents and caring adults.**

   Head to OneCaringAdult.com to access training tools and sign up for our newsletter. We cover a variety of issues, including:

   What Your Teen Is Unknowingly Trying to Tell You When They Act Out

   The #1 Mistake Parents Unintentionally Make That Causes Their Teen to Resent Them (And How to Avoid It So They Respect You Instead)

   How to Reroute Your Teen's Current Greatest Weakness into the Very Thing Responsible for Their Success

2. **Request me to speak at your school or event.**

   I've spoken to more than two million students, parents, teachers, and caring adults worldwide. My message is a unique combination of heart, humor, and practical strategies. If you'd like to request me (or one of my hand-selected speakers) to join an event, please visit TopYouthSpeakers.com.

3. **Become a youth speaker yourself.**

If you're someone who has an earnest message to share with kids or parents, this is for you. To get started, sign up for our training at YouthSpeakerU.com, and I'll share step-by-step instructions on how to make an impact through speaking.

ACKNOWLEDGMENTS

Dear Esteemed Reader,

The following is a list of smart/attractive/delightful/supportive folks you probably don't know, along with a list of inside jokes you probably won't get.

You have my full permission to understandably skip this section.

Sarah Shipp: You are seriously the best. Prima.

London: Expecto Patronum.

Katie: You're my girl.

Rodney and Christine Weidenmaier: You guys taught me all of this.

Alex and Roxanne Petruncola: Thank you for welcoming me with open arms.

Top Youth Speakers: Your impact is my greatest career highlight.

Harper Wave: Thanks for your belief from the onset and unwavering dedication.

David A. Tieche: Your insights on Trends and Challenges for Work in the 21st Century are unmatched.

Megan Bate: Thank you, Senator.

Brandon Spinnazola: You're the man.

Xander Castro: DOUBLES!!!

Travis Tindell: Beard jokes for days.

Jed Wallace: Love ya, brother.

John Wooten: Every acknowledgment is one . . .

Pacchione, Reeves, Wenzel: LaCroix en route.

Ryan Schwartz: You, sir, are a sorcerer with a quill pen.

Chandler Bolt: The subtitle is your fault.

Jamie Oliver: Thanks for lighting the path.

Dave Ramsey: Thanks for the wisdom and guidance.

To my wife's large, loving, and loud Italian family: I adore each of you. And I still am not sure who's an actual relative.

Clint Pardoe: 6–4–3 double play.

Joshua Wayne: Ready for 8 miles?

Tara Gilbert: Thanks for keeping us sane.

Gary Jones: Thanks for all the fishing trips.

Kathy McRice: We love you and miss you.

Jeff Wootton: Griffey. You're going down.

Tuesday Night Inc: Iron sharpens iron.

5AM Running Crew: Thank you for the miles and friendship.

Eric Diaz: I donut know how to thank you.

Sir Marc: FWI you're awesome.

Erin Niumata: Thanks for your constant belief and support.

Cal Z: Charles is proud of you and so am I.

Jon Talbert: Si.

Westgate: It's an honor to be a part of your community.

Daniel Harrison: Quick draw on Twitter.

Reggie Joiner & Kristen Ivy: I love the Orange Mafia and the two of you.

NOTES

1. "Key Concepts: Resilience," Harvard University Center on the Developing Child, accessed March 8, 2017, http://developingchild.harvard.edu/science/key-concepts/resilience/.

2. Global Strategy Group, "Talking With Teens: The YMCA Parent and Teen Survey Final Report," accessed March 8, 2017, http://ncfy.acf.hhs.gov/library/2000/talking-teens-ymca-parent-and-teen-survey-final-report.

3. "Talking With Teens: The YMCA Parent and Teen Survey Final Report," The White House Conference on Teenagers, accessed March 8, 2017, http://clinton4.nara.gov/WH/EOP/First_Lady/html/teens/survey.html.

4. Peter L. Benson, *All Kids Are Our Kids: What Communities Must Do to Raise Caring and Responsible Children and Adolescents* (San Francisco: Jossey-Bass, 1997), 157.

5. C. B. Lam, S. M. McHale, and A. C. Crouter, "Parent-Child Shared Time from Middle Childhood to Late Adolescence: Developmental Course and Adjustment Correlates," *Child Development* 83 (2012): 2089.

6. "How Not to Be Poor," National Center for Policy Analysis, accessed March 8, 2017, http://www.ncpa.org/pub/ba428#sthash.3u5nIAMJ.dpuf.

7. A. E. Becker, R. A. Burwell, D. B. Herzog, P. Hamburg, and S. E. Gilman, "Eating Behaviours and Attitudes Following Prolonged Exposure to Television Among Ethnic Fijian Adolescent Girls," *British Journal of Psychiatry* 180 (2002): 509–514, accessed March 8, 2017, doi: 10.1192/bjp.180.6.509.

8. Erica Goode, "Study Finds TV Alters Fiji Girls' View of Body," *New York Times*, May 20, 1999, accessed March 8, 2017, http://www.nytimes.com/1999/05/20/world/study-finds-tv-alters-fiji-girls-view-of-body.html.

9. D. Neumark-Sztainer, M. Wall, J. Haines, M. Story, and M. E. Eisenberg, "Why Does Dieting Predict Weight Gain in Adolescents? Findings from Project EAT-II: A 5-year Longitudinal Study." *Journal of the American Dietetic Association* 107(3) (2007): 448–455.

10. C. M. Shisslak, M. Crago, and L. S. Estes, "The Spectrum of Eating Disturbances." *International Journal of Eating Disorders* 18(3) (1995): 209–219.

11. F. Grodstein et al., "Three-Year Follow-Up of Participants in a Commercial Weight Loss Program: Can You Keep It Off?" *Archives of Internal Medicine* 156(12) (1996): 1302.

12. "Treatment Statistics," National Institute on Drug Abuse, accessed March 8, 2017, https://www.drugabuse.gov/publications/drugfacts/treatment-statistics.

13. Robin Barnett, *Addict in the House: A No-Nonsense Family Guide Through Addiction and Recovery* (Oakland: New Harbinger Publications, 2016), 132.

14. Lenny Bernstein, "Why a Bag of Heroin Costs Less Than a Pack of Cigarettes," *Washington Post*, August 27, 2015, accessed March 8, 2017, https://www.washingtonpost.com/news/to-your-health/wp/2015/08/27/why-a-bag-of-heroin-costs-less-than-a-pack-of-cigarettes-2/.

15. "Preventing Drug Use Among Children and Adolescents (In Brief)," National Institute on Drug Abuse, accessed March 8, 2017, https://www.drugabuse.gov/publications/preventing-drug-abuse-among-children-adolescents-in-brief/prevention-principles.

16. "Youth Risk Behavior Surveillance System," Centers for Disease Control and Prevention, accessed March 8, 2017, http://www.cdc.gov/healthyyouth/data/yrbs/index.htm.

17. Dr. Gene Beresin, Clay Center for Young Healthy Minds at Massachusetts General Hospital, a Harvard Medical School Affiliate.

18. J. Peterson, S. Freedenthal, C. Sheldon, and R. Andersen, "Nonsuicidal Self Injury in Adolescents," *Psychiatry* 5(11) (2008): 20–26, accessed March 8, 2017, https://www.ncbi.nlm.nih.gov/pmc/articles/PMC2695720/.

19. "Adolescent Self-Harm," American Association for Marriage and Family Therapy, accessed March 8, 2017, http://www.aamft.org/iMIS15/AAMFT/Content/consumer_updates/adolescent_self_harm.aspx.

20. Ted Boscia, "Study: Self-Injury in Young People Is a Gateway to Suicide," *Cornell Chronicle*, accessed March 8, 2017, http://www.news.cornell.edu/stories/2012/12/self-injury-young-people-gateway-suicide.

21. "Any Anxiety Disorder Among Children," National Institute of Mental Health, accessed March 8, 2017, https://www.nimh.nih.gov/health/statistics/prevalence/any-anxiety-disorder-among-children.shtml.

22. K. Beesdo, S. Knappe, and D. S. Pine, "Anxiety and Anxiety Disorders in Children and Adolescents: Developmental Issues and Implications for DSM-V," *Psychiatric Clinics of North America* 32 (2009): 483–524, accessed March 8, 2017, doi: 10.1016/j.psc.2009.06.002.

23. A Kaiser Family Foundation Study, "Generation M2: Media in the Lives of 8-to 18-Year-Olds," Kaiser Family Foundation, January 2010, accessed March 8, 2017, https://kaiserfamilyfoundation.files.wordpress.com/2013/04/8010.pdf.

24. Hayley Tsukayama, "Teens Spend Nearly Nine Hours Every Day Consuming Media," *Washington Post*, November 3, 2015, accessed March 8, 2017, https://

www.washingtonpost.com/news/the-switch/wp/2015/11/03/teens-spend
-nearly-nine-hours-every-day-consuming-media/.

25. Amanda Lenhart, "Teens, Social Media & Technology Overview 2015," Pew
Research Center, April 9, 2015, accessed March 8, 2017, http://www.pewin
ternet.org/2015/04/09/teens-social-media-technology-2015/.

26. "Cyber Bullying Statistics," NoBullying.com, October 19, 2016, accessed
March 8, 2017, https://nobullying.com/cyber-bullying-statistics-2014/.

27. Elizabeth K. Englander, "Research Findings: MARC 2011 Survey Grades
3–12," *MARC Research Reports*, accessed March 8, 2017, https://cdn.theatlantic
.com/static/mt/assets/science/Research%20Findings_%20MARC%202011
%20Survey%20Grades%203–12.pdf.

28. "Cyber Bullying Statistics," NoBullying.com, October 19, 2016, accessed
March 8, 2017, https://nobullying.com/cyber-bullying-statistics-2014/. NOTE:
This information is not fully verified.

29. W. E. Copeland, D. Wolke, A. Angold, and E. J. Costello, "Adult Psychiatric
and Suicide Outcomes of Bullying and Being Bullied by Peers in Childhood
and Adolescence," *JAMA Psychiatry* 70(4) (2013): 419–426, accessed March 8,
2017, doi: 10.1001/jamapsychiatry.2013.504.

30. Richard Fry, "Cumulative Student Debt Among Recent College Graduates,"
Pew Research Center, accessed March 8, 2017, http://www.pewsocialtrends
.org/2014/10/07/cumulative-student-debt-among-recent-college-graduates/.

31. "A Look at the Shocking Student Loan Debt Statistics for 2017," Student Loan
Hero, accessed March 8, 2017, https://studentloanhero.com/student-loan
-debt-statistics/.

32. Richard Fry, "Cumulative Student Debt Among Recent College Graduates,"
Pew Research Center, accessed March 8, 2017, http://www.pewsocialtrends
.org/2014/10/07/cumulative-student-debt-among-recent-college-graduates/.

33. "Quarterly Report on Household Debt and Credit," Federal Reserve Bank of
New York, August 2016, accessed March 8, 2017, https://www.newyorkfed
.org/medialibrary/interactives/householdcredit/data/pdf/HHDC_2016Q2
.pdf.

34. https://www.newyorkfed.org/medialibrary/interactives/householdcredit
/data/xls/sl_update_2016.xlsx.

35. "Is There a Student Loan Crisis? Not in Payments," *Forefront*, Federal Reserve Bank of Cleveland, May 16, 2016, accessed March 8, 2017, https://
clevelandfed.org/newsroom-and-events/publications/forefront/ff-v7n02/ff
-20160516-v7n0204-is-there-a-student-loan-crisis.aspx.

36. Research even suggests this pithy saying has some truth to it: Sarah Millar,
"Why You're Only As Happy As Your Least Happy Child," *Toronto Star*, August 31, 2011, accessed March 8, 2017, https://www.thestar.com/life/health
_wellness/2011/08/31/why_youre_only_as_happy_as_your_least_happy_child
.html.

37. Mary Holsopple. Presentation at "Bullying 101," accredited pre-conference, IBPA Conference, Nashville, Tennessee, November 10, 2013. Holsopple quoted information from T. Vaillancourt et al., "Peer Victimization, Depressive Symptoms, and High Salivary Cortisol Predict Poorer Memory in Children." *Brain Cognition Journal* 77(2) (2011): 191–99.

38. Deborah Lessne and Melissa Cidade of Synergy Enterprises, "Student Reports of Bullying and Cyber-Bullying: Results from the 2013 School Crime Supplement to the National Crime Victimization Survey," National Center for Education Statistics, April 2015, accessed March 8, 2017, http://nces.ed .gov/pubsearch/pubsinfo.asp?pubid=2015056.

39. "The Bully Prevention Primer," *Christian Educators Journal*, accessed March 8, 2017, http://www.cejonline.com/article/the-bully-prevention-primer/.

40. D. L. Hawkins, D. J. Pepler, and W. M. Craig, "Naturalistic Observations of Peer Interventions in Bullying," *Social Development* 10 (2001): 512–527, accessed March 8, 2017, http://bullylab.com/Portals/0/Naturalistic%20 observations%20of%20peer%20interventions%20in%20bullying.pdf.

41. Survey of 14,000 high school students done by the Massachusetts Aggression Reduction Center at Bridgewater State University.

42. "From Teasing to Torment: School Climate Revisited," GLSEN, accessed March 8, 2017, https://www.glsen.org/sites/default/files/TeasingtoTorment %202015%20FINAL%20PDF%5B1%5D_0.pdf.

43. "Fast Facts: Bullying," National Center for Education Statistics, accessed March 8, 2017, https://nces.ed.gov/fastfacts/display.asp?id=719.

44. Letters from the Education Secretary or Deputy Secretary, US Department of Education, December 31, 2015, accessed March 8, 2017, http://www2.ed .gov/policy/gen/guid/secletter/151231.html.

Josh Shipp helps adults understand teens and teens understand themselves. He is a global youth empowerment expert and an acclaimed speaker. He has appeared on MTV, Lifetime, *Oprah*, CNN, FOX, *20/20*, *Good Morning America*, and in the *New York Times* and other media. A former at-risk foster kid turned youth advocate, he is renowned for his documentary TV series that followed his groundbreaking work with teens. His organization, One Caring Adult, produces resources and training events for parents, educators, and caring adults. Visit OneCaringAdult.com to learn more and for free resources.